Recent Research in Psychology

Marshall J. Farr

The Long-Term Retention of Knowledge and Skills

A Cognitive and Instructional Perspective

Springer-Verlag
New York Berlin Heidelberg
London Paris Tokyo

Marshall J. Farr
2520 North Vernon Street
Arlington, Virginia 22207

Library of Congress Cataloging in Publication Data
Farr, Marshall J.
  The long-term retention of knowledge and skills.
  (Recent research in psychology)
  "Prepared for the Under Secretary of Defense for
Research and Engineering, U.S. Department of Defense,
and the Institute for Defense Analyses "IDA",
Alexandria, Virginia"—
  1. Memory. 2. Learning, Psychology of.
I. United States. Office of the Under Secretary of
Defense for Research and Engineering. II. Institute
for Defense Analyses. III. Title. IV. Series.
BF371.F28 1987 153.1'2 87-9737

The material herein was originally prepared for the Institute for Defense Analyses (IDA), Alexandria, Virginia, in support of the Under Secretary of Defense for Research and Engineering, U.S. Department of Defense, as part of their focus on the improvement of training. The material was originally issued as IDA Memorandum Report M-205, September 1986.

Printed and bound by Edwards Brothers, Incorporated, Ann Arbor, Michigan.
Printed in the United States of America.

9 8 7 6 5 4 3 2 1

ISBN 0-387-96531-9 Springer-Verlag New York Berlin Heidelberg
ISBN 3-540-96531-9 Springer-Verlag Berlin Heidelberg New York

CONTENTS

TABLES

ABBREVIATIONS

AI	Artificial Intelligence
ARI	Army Research Institute for the Behavioral and Social Sciences
ASVAB	Armed Services Vocational Aptitude Battery
ATI	Aptitude-treatment interaction
CAI	Computer-assisted instruction
CMI	Computer-managed instruction
EPC	Expended-processing capacity
KRRS	Knowledge-representation/retrieval structure
K&S	Knowledge and skills
LOP	Level of processing
LTR	Long-term retention
LTS	Long-term store
NPRDC	Navy Personnel Research and Development Center
OL	Original learning
R&D	Research and development
STM	Short-term memory
STS	Short-term store
TBL	To-be-learned
UDA	User's Decision Aid

SUMMARY

A. INTRODUCTION AND BACKGROUND[1,2]

This report reviews and interprets research on the nature and magnitude of the effects of those factors which influence how well knowledge and skills (K&S) are retained over relatively long periods of nonuse. Our interest lies in the kinds of knowledge domains and skills that military personnel must master to function effectively on their jobs. The practical concern impelling this study is that K&S degradation or loss (which we will refer to as "decay") can and does occur, often and severely enough, to jeopardize military preparedness. There are occasions in all the military services when personnel who have just completed their training do not receive an opportunity to practice or use their new capabilities for weeks or months. In the case of reservists who may be called back to active duty, the period of nonuse of relevant military job skills may be counted in terms of years.

B. OBJECTIVES

The overall objective is to critically analyze the relevant scientific literature which relates the processes involved in learning to those of memory, taking into account the characteristics of the learner and the learning tasks. More specifically, we have focused on the following sub-objectives:

1. Identify, describe and rank the influence and the interactions of the important major variables that affect long-term retention (LTR);

---

[1] I am indebted to Dr. Jesse Orlansky, Institute for Defense Analyses, for his encouragement and guidance through all phases of this report. Thanks are also given to Drs. Martin A. Tolcott, Norman E. Lane and Richard S. Gibson for their helpful comments.

[2] This work was performed under Task T-5-310, Cost-Effectiveness Methods for Assessing Training Technologies. Technical cognizance was provided by Captain Paul R. Chatelier, the Military Assistant for Training and Personnel Technology, DUSD(R&AT).

2. Apply the latest relevant theoretical formulations (which, for the most part, reflect contemporary viewpoints in experimental cognitive psychology) towards new and novel interpretions of how and why these variables exert their effect on storage and retrieval;

3. Identify task characteristics which are most likely to lead to forgetting;

4. Identify instructional strategies (conditions of learning) which promote LTR, but do not adversely impact on learning or facilitative transfer.

5. Identify techniques for predicting the amount of K&S decay for various periods of nonuse.

6. Recommend realistic, potentially cost-effective approaches to retarding the decay attributable to little use or nonuse of learned K&S.

7. Suggest an R&D agendum to fill in the gaps and to explore new directions deriving from the theoretical insights gained by this review.

C. SCOPE AND APPROACH

Our scope spans the full range of types of tasks, skills and knowledge domains, populations of different abilities and a variety of contexts. It samples key studies, experimental and naturalistic, from basic laboratory research to applied settings in the "dirty," real world of the military. This broad coverage derives from (a) our belief that basic and applied findings, from the psychology laboratory and from the educational researcher concerned with school subjects and classroom conditions, can lead to important theoretical and practical advances; and (b) the fact that there is a relative scarcity of research directly dealing with or relevant to military populations, tasks and training conditions.

To be as comprehensive as possible, within the practical constraints of time and resources, we have analyzed prior reviews, dealing with LTR, issued from 1962 to 1983. We extracted from these reviews the factors differentiated as being most indicative of the course of K&S degradation. For each factor, we suggest a rating, based on the evidence in each review, of its strength of effect, i.e., how much it contributes to the LTR of the K&S involved. In addition to evaluating the review articles, we also analyze relatively recent, prototypical or seminal experiments relevant to the important influential variables.

1. The Cognitive Perspective

Our review led us to conclude that most relevant scientific studies were methodologically flawed, lacking a common metric for measuring the degree of learning and the rate of forgetting, and deficient in theoretical derivation or interpretation. We therefore applied a cognitively oriented interpretation to prior findings and prevailing beliefs about the nature of LTR. The cognitive point of view regards the learner as someone who actively transforms all perceptions (by encoding or processing them) from the raw (unprocessed) sensory-level to meaningful material compatible with what the individual already knows (that is frequently referred to as his world knowledge).

The extent to which information is "deeply" or "strongly" or elaboratively *processed* determines the way it is organized and, consequently, represented in memory for subsequent retrieval. The analogy here (admittedly oversimplified) is to an efficient office or library filing system. If that system contains a large number and variety of meaningful and relevant file terms, all cross-referenced to each other, one can more readily locate what one is searching for, even with only imprecise or ambiguous descriptor terms or cues available.

2. Theory and Issues

The two main theories as to why forgetting occurs are those of Trace Decay and Interference with the retrieval process. The Trace view holds that every sensation or event which is strong enough to register and be cognitively processed leaves an organic residual effect called a memory trace. A set of related events or concurrent stimuli may result in a complex, multi-attribute, multi-layered trace. We call the mental representation of the knowledge which the trace stands for the Knowledge-Representation/Retrieval Structure (KRRS). In order for successful remembering to occur, a selective *retrieval* process must be posited, involving locating and contacting (collectively called *accessing*) the target trace, which is part of a KRRS containing related and associated information.

Forgetting can be explained as due to (a) a weakened trace or KRRS; and/or (b) interference with the retrieval of the trace, resulting from similar material, either incoming or already stored, being mistaken for the correct trace. There is no reason why both possible explanations of forgetting might not apply in any particular case. In fact, we hold the view that different components of the KRRS may "decay" at different rates. We do not use the term "decay" here to mean that some organic change has occurred. Rather, we merely mean that, as time passes and as different component traces of a KRRS are accessed differentially, the "exercised" components are made less vulnerable to decay. On the other hand, the component trace not accessed receives no practice and tends to get functionally weaker and more difficult to recover.

3. Relationships Between Acquisition and Retention

The separation between the learning phase and the retention phase is arbitrary, in the sense that we can only determine whether a person has successfully learned something by having him demonstrate its retention. Furthermore, the criterion for when learning has been achieved (which we call the mastery criterion) is also often arbitrary, whether in the experimental laboratory or the classroom. When someone continues receiving learning trials beyond the point of initial mastery, we define this as "overlearning." This kind of overlearning, achieved by practice or rehearsal after mastery has been demonstrated, is the usual way of increasing the degree or strength of original learning (OL). There are, however, other methods which have in common the requirement that the learner has to process the to-be-learned material more intensively and/or extensively than usual in order to make it more meaningful, better organized, and/or more distinctive. For example, the learner may have to process a stimulus which is incomplete or otherwise degraded before he can correctly recognize the stimulus object and commit it to memory. Such *enhanced* processing, the literature reveals, is likely to promote both acquisition and LTR.

D. CONCLUSIONS AS TO MAJOR VARIABLES INFLUENCING LONG-TERM RETENTION

Of the key factors that importantly affect the course of retention, we identify below those that have been the typical variables of most empirical studies. The general consensus of the major reviewers, plus our own judgement of the experimental literature, support the order, based on the influence of these variables, in which we consider them. The one exerting the strongest, i.e., most reliably predictable, effect is discussed first. The rest follow in descending order of influence. However, this ordering should be interpreted cautiously for a good number of reasons. Chief among these are: (a) some variables are so global that they really represent several sub-variables which do not affect LTR equally, e.g., the instructional strategy employed; (b) some variables, such as the length of the retention interval, typically interact with other variables; and (c) the effect of a variable can be markedly changed if we change the method of measuring retention, e.g., from recognition to recall.

1.   Variable: The Degree of Original Learning

There is almost unanimous agreement that the single most important determinant of both knowledge and skill retention is the amount or degree of initial learning. As pointed out above, overlearning can increase this amount or degree. It therefore follows plausibly, and the experimental evidence supports it, that decay can be reduced and delayed by overlearning or by enhanced learning. The cautionary note here is that increased amounts of overlearning facilitate retention at a decreasing rate, sometimes reaching a point of negligible advantage as compared to a lesser degree of original learning.

2.   Variable: Task Characteristics (Type and Complexity of Organization)

a. Continuous-control tasks, exemplified by a motor task such as tracking, are better retained, even for extended time periods (months or years) than discrete or procedural tasks (usually verbally mediated or executed).

b. The "complexity" of a task, i.e., its degree of organization or cohesiveness, either inherent or imposed by the learner, appears to be the dominant operative characteristic that determines both acquisition and LTR. The more cohesive or integrated a task is, or the more inherently amenable it is to learner-imposed organization, the less it will decay. This conclusion clearly applies to the evidence that complex procedural skills are highly subject to forgetting, even after relatively short periods of nonuse. A point to appreciate: Procedural tasks are the types of tasks military enlisted personnel are most often required to learn.

3.   Variable: Retention Interval

a. In general, the longer the period of nonuse, the greater will be the decay. However, the *amount* of decay is quite sensitive to the task characteristics, degree of original learning and method of training.

b. The *rate* of decay can be different for different skills or components of a multi-component task, such as a procedural task with many steps.

c. Forgetting or skill decay during the retention interval can be reduced by a relatively small investment in mental rehearsal or "imaginary practice."

4. Variable: Instructional Strategies/Conditions of Learning

a. Programmed instruction, which usually is used for training verbal or intellectual skills (as opposed to motor skills) leads to better retention than conventional (platform-based, lock-step) instruction if the "acquisition is good."

b. Feedback which gives the trainee enough information to understand and correct his errors is essential to learning and retention.

c. Based upon the research literature dealing with the learning of meaningful connected discourse (known as prose or text learning), the degree to which material to be learned receives *elaborative processing* determines, in large part, how well it will be learned, retained and transferred. What is not adequately known is how best to design or deliver instruction which induces the most effective elaborative processing (generically termed *enhanced* processing).

5. Variable: Methods for Testing Retention/Conditions of Retrieval

a. Different retention measures can yield different degrees of apparent retention. For example, free-recall responses required by a retention test usually yield lower scores that a recognition (e.g., multiple-choice) test. A cautionary note follows: When comparing the effectiveness of different variables for increasing LTR, one should make certain that the same retention technique has been employed.

b. Skill retention scores will be increased if the retention measurement is conducted in a context similar to that of the original learning.

c. For motor skills, the time saved in *relearning* to the original mastery criterion is generally more than 50%.

6. Variable: Individual Differences

a. There has been very little research directed at the relationship between LTR and individual-differences variables (e.g., in ability, prior knowledge, and motivation). Most conclusions about the role of this variable in LTR derive *indirectly* from its relation to acquisition. The literature concludes that higher-ability learners (as measured by the

ASVAB) tend to reach a higher degree of original learning, and thus retain more, than lower-ability individuals.

b. There is some evidence that lower-ability learners forget a larger proportion of abstract, theoretical material than do higher-ability individuals. This seems quite plausible, since this kind of material demands the kind of superior information processing and problem-solving capabilities that those with greater ability would have, as compared to less able learners. The more able people would form more intensively processed and, therefore, more retrievable traces. And their better understanding of the theoretical relationships would allow them to "regenerate" memories lost to the less able individual.

E. SELECTED SUPPLEMENTARY CONCLUSIONS

The conclusions in this section comprise only a selected set, since we have presented a larger number above as they derive from the major variables typically investigated in the relevant literature. The conclusions below, which may overlap slightly with those already presented, were chosen because they are more sweeping in scope, more general, and can thus serve more readily as the basis for prescriptive recommendations to promote LTR.

1. Learning/Training Conditions

a. The greater the degree to which the learner has mastered the K or S, the slower will be the rate of decay. This degree of learning or mastery is usually increased by having the learner gain more practice with the material (called overlearning). It can also be increased by inducing the trainee to more deeply and extensively process the material, e.g., in order to overcome interference.

b. The "quality" (as contrasted to the "strength") of the memory traces formed while learning is probably the single most important determinant of LTR, especially for complex and/or difficult tasks. This quality is a function of the degree and kind of cognitive processing performed on the to-be-learned material. It can be increased through appropriate instructional design and strategies.

c. LTR will increase the more that the context of the training environment and conditions of training resemble the job or real-world environment in which the learned K or S will be applied.

d. The more that the learner can meaningfully integrate new incoming information with his existing knowledge structures, the better the new information will be remembered. Maximal integration which will most benefit both acquisition and LTR occurs when the new information is *understood* in terms of what the learner *already* comprehends.

e. Since memory is largely reconstructive, we should, wherever applicable, teach concepts, principles and rules to complement or supplement teaching rote knowledge or facts. This will promote effective understanding of a task domain and thus allow the learner to later generate or regenerate details which would not otherwise be available to memory.

2. Characteristics of the Task

a. Certain attributes of a task, which essentially represent its complexity and "difficulty," can be analyzed to yield a kind of task-characteristic *memorability* measure. This measure can be successfully used, particularly for relatively simple procedural tasks, to predict how much the task will decay over any given interval of nonuse.

b. Different components (subtasks, steps) of a complex task (defined generally as a task which may tap different abilities, require reasoning or problem solving, and/or contain multiple, interrelated facts or concepts) will decay over time at different rates. Attempts to assign these kinds of tasks a single, robust decay-rate predictor would seem fruitless.

c. In learning from prose or text, different kinds of information (e.g., paragraph theme, sentence gist and sentence wording) yield different retention curves. These findings could stem from different kinds and degrees of processing of these different attributes.

d. Skills (such as typing or reading) which have become more highly organized, cohesive, proceduralized or automated through extensive practice show negligible decay over long periods of nonuse.

3. Predicting the Course of Retention During Nonuse Intervals

a. The approximate rate of decay can be predicted for certain kinds of tasks (typically, procedural in nature) whose components are organizationally related to each other and to the total task in a relatively straightforward manner.

b. Two Army-sponsored studies done since 1980 report that they have successfully used an algorithm, based on mathematical learning theory, to predict the percent of military procedural task decay over given periods of time. The input data for the algorithm come from the individual's performance on his *first* learning trial.

F. RECOMMENDATIONS/PRESCRIPTIONS FOR INCREASING LTR

Although there is necessarily some overlap with the Conclusions we have presented above, this section attempts to summarize, briefly, actual steps that can be taken to either directly promote LTR by some training intervention, or slow down the rate of decay by intervention during the nonuse retention period.

1. Training Task Analysis

a. A training task analysis (performed to aid in designing an instructional system) should carefully consider the recall context (the operational or real-world environment in which the learner must function) and the possible cuing stimuli that may be present.

b. The training task analysis should rate the memorability of the various task characteristics. With these measures, it might be possible to selectively "overtrain" the less memorable attributes so that their specific retention curves could be improved.

2. Instructional Strategies/Conditions of Learning

a. Design instruction which causes the learner to *process* the material to be learned at an *enhanced* level. This typically involves providing elaborative associations, advance organizers, topical headings, and the like.

b. Wherever possible, if concepts and relationships are part of what is to be learned, directly teach and test *understanding*, as contrasted to any rote-memory components. The understanding (a) provides a meaningful ideational scaffolding to hold together and cue the components; and (b) facilitates positive transfer.

c. For critical tasks where it is especially important that performance be errorless, stable and durable, "overtrain" the learners by increasing the required mastery-criterion level, or by inducing the learner to process the material both more intensively and extensively.

d. For tasks (such as procedures) which mainly involve discrete component steps that flow sequentially, add elaborative verbal or imaginal linking associations to each step that does not provide intrinsic cuing to its immediately following step.

e. Where unrelated facts or rote material are to be learned, mnemonic devices, such as acronyms or unusual imaginal associations, can be inserted to aid the learner to create a more distinctive and, hence, accessible trace.

f. Allow the higher-ability learners to set their own pace, but provide them with relatively well-designed material structured to promote enhanced processing and, consequently, more durable memory. We are thus recommending individualized instruction in the sense of pace, but not in the sense of choosing one's own path through the course of learning.

3. **Counteracting Memory Decay During Nonuse Periods**

a. "Imaginary" or covert rehearsal can prove effective in retarding decay. Thus, during periods of nonuse, have the trainee mentally rehearse or act out the skill or the knowledge learned.

b. If we are dealing with a simple, or a well-organized complex task, we need to provide only occasional practice and short periods of rehearsal to sustain the task or skill. This has particular significance for the use of part-task simulators to provide this more limited and cheaper training.

c. Procedural skills can be quickly relearned, without having actually to execute the procedure, by studying written jobs aids or reminder material such as technical manuals.

d. A low-cost equivalent of refresher training can be provided by *testing* the learner, especially using tests of the hands-on, performance-type when applicable. An added benefit is that the test results can be used for diagnostic and evaluative purposes.

4. Fidelity of Simulation

a. Where complex, abstract relationships among systems, functions, phenomena, equipment, etc., must be taught, there need be only that degree of simulation of the physical system and its parts sufficient to induce mental representations of the relationships. The fidelity required for this *conceptual* simulation can be much lower than for full-scale simulation.

b. Practice on even one aspect or part of a task can be potent enough to reinstate the entire task. Existing part-task simulators might be used effectively to provide this practice.

G. ISSUES FOR FURTHER RESEARCH AND DEVELOPMENT

A number of areas and issues deserve further research and development. These range from theory-building and hypotheses-testing to practical, applied, quite focused research. The descriptions below start with the more basic-research concerns and end with the more applied concerns.

1. How "motor memory" is represented in trace form.

2. The relationship of individual differences to LTR.

3. A more precise, preferably objectively or operationally measurable, index of "how much" learning has taken place. This will, among other things, allow us to compare across individuals, and to have a common point from which to measure the course of retention.

4. What are the *qualitative* effects of overlearning for different kinds of complex tasks? This relates to the fundamental question of whether sheer repetition, as opposed to strategic cognitive processing, promotes more durable memory.

5. (Related to the prior item.) How do we measure the *quality* of what one has learned as opposed to the amount or magnitude? (We know that, as one learns complex, meaningful material, the abilities required change, insight occurs, understanding develops, etc.) The "quality" index may well be more predictive of LTR and facilitative transfer than any quantitative measure.

6. (Related to the prior two items.) We need operational definitions (supported by empirical evidence) of the "distinctiveness" or the "discriminability" of memory traces. This knowledge is essential if we are to develop a prescriptive science of instruction. These characteristics of traces have been conclusively associated with increased memorability.

7. How do we definably and reliably increase the degree or level of original learning (and thereby improve LTR) without having to unaffordably increase the time spent in the acquisition phase? This relates to a very practical concern: What is the trade-off between time spent in the acquisition phase and decreased need for refresher training.

8. In organizing instruction so as to achieve enhanced processing and the resultant improved memorability, is it more effective to encourage the learner to form his *own* enriched memory encodings, or to provide him with all of the elaborative material?

9. We need an operational definition of task complexity that will inform us of both the memorability of the total task and its components taken *individually*. We further require a means for deriving an index, preferably a quantitative one, that we can effectively use for twin purposes:

(a) for determining the ease of learning the task; and

(b) for predicting the decay rate of the task or any of its major components.

10. There is some evidence that the instructional needs for relearning (refresher training) are different than those for original learning. To what extent, and how, can we "abbreviate" or "streamline" the degree and kind of instruction needed for refresher training?

11. We need to develop a model, algorithm or equation which will predict the course of decay over time, for all types of tasks, as a function of the cognitive demands of the learning task, the conditions of learning, and the shape and end point of each individual's learning curve.

I. INTRODUCTION

The Department of Defense is concerned, from an overall, practical point of view, with improving the "life-cycle training" of military personnel. Such an approach to training effectiveness must consider not only how to achieve more rapid, higher-quality training, but also (a) how well that training will endure, that is, how resistant it will be to infrequent or nonuse of the knowledge and skills (K&S) acquired; and (b) how adequately the training (typically classroom or simulator-based) will prepare the individual for the real-world, job environment. This reports deals primarily with what happens to the products of learning *after* they have been acquired. Typically, of course, this means that the forgetting process sets in.

Lane (in press), in a recent review that focused on the *acquisition* process noted that, although the psychological and educational literature presents *group* learning and forgetting curves for some broad, taxonomic categories of tasks (e.g., from nonsense-syllable lists to motor learning), there is surprisingly and disappointingly little in the literature of practical use to the learning and retention of the broad range of complex, real-world "cognitive" tasks. [Two notable exceptions, which will be covered in detail later, are relatively recent empirical programs by the Army Research Institute (ARI) (see Hagman and Rose, 1983) and the Navy Personnel Research & Development Center (NPRDC) (see Konoske and Ellis, 1985).]

The case for the importance of improving education and training in society in general and the military in particular is obvious. The U.S. military probably run the largest single training enterprise in the free world. But, unlike our public educational system, with its emphasis on academic, not vocational, skills, the armed forces train their personnel so that they can effectively use their acquired K&S on the job or in pursuit of advanced or related training. It follows that what has been acquired has to be retained for some considerable time, and should be able to be successfully transferred or applied to a variety of tasks and job skills related to the specific set of K&S learned by the individual.

1

Perhaps the most basic common-sense datum we all believe in, because we have all experienced it, is that knowledge is forgotten and that skills deteriorate if not used or practiced to some degree. Unfortunately, the complexities of military operations, recruit-accession practices and other practical-scheduling factors make it difficult to provide personnel with adequate opportunities to use (and thus maintain) their learned K&S. Some of the tasks for which someone is trained may not be called for on the job right away. Skills which are learned early in a lengthy course may become degraded even before the course is over. Reserve military personnel may not get the right amount, quality and frequency of practice to sustain their skills.

As both enlisted and officer training come to deal with more technologically advanced and intellectually demanding jobs, the importance of effective and durable training can only increase. When economic conditions and a dwindling supply of available personnel of qualified military age resurrect the need to accept more lower-ability personnel, the training of these individuals may present special problems. There is already some suggestive evidence (as we shall see later when we discuss individual differences) that these lower-ability trainees tend to forget more of what they've learned than their more able colleagues. We will certainly need training strategies particularly appropriate to the needs of these lower-level individuals.

All in all, we need to know a great deal more of useful information about the factors which promote long-term retention (LTR) and retard "decay." (We will use the term "skill decay" or just "decay" as a shortcut convenience to mean any deterioration in skill or loss of knowledge following K&S acquisition. The use of the term does not imply that we endorse any particular theory of forgetting, such as the literal meaning of the word would suggest.)

2

II. OBJECTIVES/DESIRED END PRODUCTS

The literature on *long-term* retention of K&S, ranging from a one-day to a 50-year time interval (see, for example, Bahrick, 1984) is particularly sparse in relating acquisition data meaningfully to the *quality*, as well as to the durability, of what has been mastered. The *quality* of learning is a uniquely important attribute which has been relatively neglected by those researchers studying *long-term* memory in order to influence or to predict the course of forgetting. There has been some recognition, in recent years, by those concerned with the acquisition and *short-duration* retention of verbal prose material, of the *qualitative* aspects of the learning process (see Craik, 1979, for a review of some of this work). We will later develop our view of this attribute of quality as a potentially potent construct for explaining and reinterpreting some of the typical findings in the literature on LTR, especially in connection with "overlearning." If one samples the literature from a great number and variety of sources, the following picture emerges. What one usually measures to gauge whether learning has occurred is, conceptually, the *strength* of the connections or associations formed. Yet, operationally, the teacher or trainer is measuring the achievement of a particular criterion (often called a *mastery* criterion) related to acquiring a certain amount of the to-be-learned material or skill, to a set level of accuracy. Occasionally, the learning must be accomplished within some limited period of time. For example, the student is to learn a list of 25 pairs of English-French equivalent nouns so that, given only the English words as his[3] cues, he can supply the correct French words with 80% accuracy within a total of five minutes.

The quality of what someone has learned is difficult to measure. We believe that higher-quality learning usually means that the learner has *processed* the learned material to a "deeper" level (Craik & Lockhart, 1972), or in such a way that he has incorporated the new information into his existing knowledge-representation structure so that it makes more

---

[3] In the interest of avoiding awkward grammatical constructions, the pronouns *he, him* and *his* will be used to represent both genders in the absence of any gender-specific antecedent.

connections with a larger number of pre-existing memory structures. In other words, if we think for a moment of what we do in an office system for filing correspondence, billings, records of customer complaints, maintenance-of-equipment records, etc., we know that a filing system which is extensively cross-referenced will allow for quicker and more certain retrieval of desired information. In the *ideal* cross-referenced system, any reasonably relevant cue will eventually allow the searcher to locate and extract what he's seeking. This admittedly mechanistic analogy of the human memory-retrieval system to an office filing system is an oversimplification, but it serves the purpose of clarifying the concept of the quality of an information-storage system. Later in this paper, as we elaborate on this, we will debate the strength vs quality issue, discuss instructional strategies which lead to better qualitative learning, and argue that positive transfer is predominantly a function of the *quality*, rather than the *strength*, of learning.

The overall general objective of this review is to analyze all the relevant literature which *relates* acquisition-process variables to retention-process variables, taking into account the obvious influence of the characteristics of the learner and the learning tasks. More specifically, we will focus on this relationship by pursuing the following sub-objectives:

A. Identify, describe, and rank the influence of the important operative variables that affect long-term retention.

B. Specify, wherever data are available, the nature and extent of the interaction of these variables.

C. Propose empirically-supported, theory-based explanations of how these variables exert their influence on retention.

D. Identify K&S components or characteristics which are most susceptible to decay.

E. Identify instructional strategies and/or conditions of learning which promote LTR without adversely affecting either learning or facilitative transfer.

F. Identify techniques for predicting amount of K&S decay for various forgetting intervals.

4

G. Determine whether there are instructional approaches to *refresher* training which may be differentially effective in comparison to approaches used in original learning (OL).

H. Recommend realistic, potentially cost-effective approaches for dealing with the decay which results from protracted periods of inadequate or no practice after learning.

I. Suggest a basic and applied research agendum to help plug identified gaps and explore new directions stemming from fresh theoretical reinterpretations.

III. SCOPE

As we will show, most of the major literature reviews that have been conducted on this topic of long-term retention have been relatively straightforward reports on empirical findings that emphasize a specific kind of learning (for example, motor skills), or a specific domain (for example, flight skills). For the most part, they either have not reviewed, or have reviewed only a small sample, of the "academic" literature from the basic research of the experimental psychology laboratory, or the not-so-basic research of the educational researcher whose target is typically prose (i.e., verbal, continuous, meaningful text) learning.

For example, referring to Table A-1, wherein we have tried to capture succinctly the focus and scope of the seven major reviews (of *long-term* retention) published between 1961 and 1983, one can see that they were conducted with a limited set of objectives. Naylor and Briggs (1961), in what was apparently the first systematic review dedicated to skill retention, were concerned mainly with motor skills within a flight-skill-retention framework. Gardlin and Sitterley (1972) restricted themselves to reports "dealing with close to operational conditions" (p. 3). Prophet (1976), like Naylor and Briggs (1961), narrowed his focus to flying skills, even grouping them on a scale of relevancy to their memorability. Schendel, Shields and Katz (1978) centered their sights on motor skills, emphasizing findings from military research; by their own admission, they skimmed over "data relevant to a more detailed understanding of the behavioral consequences of an extended no-practice period..." (from the unpaginated "Brief" preceding the Introduction). Annett (1979) was concerned chiefly with *skills*, as contrasted to "memory for words, scenes or events" (p. 215). Hurlock and Montague (1982) list only 24 references, a highly selected sample of studies and reviews relevant to skill loss in the Navy. Finally, Hagman and Rose (1983) reviewed only thirteen experimental studies, conducted or sponsored within the last ten years or so by the U.S. Army. (We will have more to say later about this "review of reviews" and about Table A-1.)

In contrast to these reviews, the present review covers the full range of types of skills and domains, from basic laboratory research to applied studies in the "dirty" real world of the military. We take a full-width and full-depth perspective view of what is relevant to the very practical problem of improving LTR. Although our review cannot be exhaustive, it is centered selectively on all types of learning tasks and materials, populations of differing abilities, and a variety of contexts. It operates on the belief that quite basic as well as applied findings, from laboratory and non-military educational contexts, can lead, directly or indirectly, to important theoretical implications that can be heuristically valuable to explain, predict and produce improved learning and retention. We believe that the sweep, intent and combined theoretical and applied orientation of this review are needed to provide more credible and useful interpretations of the qualitative and quantitative data found in the literature.

Experimental psychology is now heavily flavored with the cognitive science/artificial-intelligence viewpoint. Similarly, educational and training practitioners and researchers are increasingly sympathetic to the movement away from conventional, platform-based instruction, and towards "high-tech" intelligent computer-program implementations of individualized, self-paced training. Yet, in spite of these converging sympathies, these two communities continue to study different kinds of learning and use different paradigmatic approaches. For the most part, they appear unaware of each other's experimental crucibles, theoretical concerns and application areas of interest.

The third community studying the relationship between learning and LTR is comprised of military researchers whose prime R&D objective is to come up with findings of obvious relevance to or, better yet, ready applicability to military problems. The military researcher, whose approach is typified by the studies reviewed by Hagman and Rose (1983), runs controlled studies of real-world typical or prototypical tasks, using military personnel in operational environments.

Each community has already produced findings of at least empirical value. The main deficit, as we see it, is that we lack an over-arching theoretical framework which can help us make sense of the ambiguous, inconsistant or inconclusive findings in this area. We will propose such a theoretical framework and try to argue successfully for its explanatory power. We believe it can point the way to (a) prescriptions for designing instruction that can promote learning, retention *and* transfer; and (b) models that can lead to implementable techniques to predict the course of retention, for the full variety and complexity of task types, more precisely than (for example) the task-retention-rating system (Rose, Radtke, Shettel & Hagman, 1985) developed for the U.S. Army. (That rating system, based upon the characteristics of the task to be learned, will be described in some detail later.)

IV. APPROACH

By this point, the reader will have gathered that we believe the literature on LTR is disappointingly fragmented, surprisingly barren of a theory-guiding framework for yielding fruitful, testable hypotheses, and of limited real-world application. As pointed out, there are essentially separate literatures resulting from researchers representing different outlooks, communities, and basic and applied requirements. When we began this review, our desire was to conduct a *meta-analysis*, which is an integrated-review approach that goes well beyond the typical chronologically-assembled, narrative description of a body of related research. Glass (1977) coined the term meta-analysis, in response to what he saw as a demand for more sophisticated techniques of measurement and statistical analysis, to describe an approach which could be applied to the accumulated findings of dozens or even hundreds of studies.

However, in spite of his plea for the extra rigor that a meta-analysis would effect, Glass wisely recognized the technique's possible pitfalls: the most serious, statistically-based criticism is that many weak studies, taken together, could add to a spurious, strong-effect conclusion. Glass acknowledged further that there are several key aspects of "faith" in applying the meta-analytic approach. For one, the variable(s) of interest "should not be so complex and varied as to permit no simple answers" (p. 365). Examples of such overly complex variables cited by Glass ranged from the "amount of psychotherapy" to "hours of instruction" (p. 362). This latter variable, he suggests, is not amenable to a meta-analysis because one cannot equate, for example, one hour a week spread over ten consecutive weeks with ten hours massed in five 2-hour sessions within a single week. As a parenthetical comment, this "hours of instruction" variable can be seen as quite analogous to the several temporal-scheduling factors that importantly influence learning and retention: exposure time, intervals between learning or relearning trials, the temporal spacing of massed vs. distributed learning trials, and the spacing of test trials interleaved with learning trials.

We make this point about the nature of variables not conducive to a meta-analysis to help explain, in part, our conclusion that the meta-analytic approach as such could not be appropriately applied to the literature on LTR. Other considerations that led us to reject the meta-analytic technique are best explained by pointing out that the relevant literature is a serious victim of two of the most important acknowledged limitations (Jackson, 1980) of the technique, namely: (a) the meta-analytic approach cannot be used to infer which characteristics of studies on a given topic *caused* the differing results; and (b) the approach suffers from the lack of common or equivalent metrics for the measures used and reported in the various studies on the topic. For example, it is not at all clear that performing a motor task without errors for the first time is equivalent, in *level* of learning, to learning a list of paired English and French nouns to what *seems* to be the same mastery criterion -- the first completely correct trial.

There are other convincing reasons for finding meta-analytic technique not suitable for our purposes. For one thing, we see the most need for the power of such an approach when the targeted research area reveals importantly different and/or apparently contradictory results. On the contrary, we find relatively little real controversy about what are the crucial, molar variables influencing LTR, and in which direction they exert their effect. (The seven major reviews we examined and analyzed [see Table A-1, which we will discuss later] testify to this observation.) For example, there is essential agreement with the conclusion that additional learning time or trials, given after "minimal" mastery or acquisition, will result in a state of "overlearning." Such a state is uniformly acknowledged to be more resistant to decay than learning which does not proceed beyond minimal mastery. What is not known empirically is *how much* "extra" retention is gained by successive definable increments of overlearning.

Suffice it to say, at this point, that the literature on overlearning (which we will be discussing later in some detail) consistently reveals that, as you increase the nonuse retention interval, the facilitative effects of certain degrees of overlearning lose some of their superiority over lesser degrees of learning. In fact, curves of retention drop off as a function of a number of variables other than the level of overlearning, e.g., different kinds of tasks, and ability differences in the learner. Even if it were feasible and affordable to gather enough data on all these influential variables for use in predictive equations, it would not answer the much more (potentially) cost-effective and theoretically significant question:

12

Is the "extra" learning that is occurring (during the trials or repetitions that take someone beyond minimal learning) changing the quality or nature of what is being learned? Is the phenomenon of overlearning increasing retention because it allows further opportunity for a deeper level of processing and more elaborate encoding? These specific questions will be the subject of extended discussion later in this paper. These *kinds* of questions not only reflect contemporary cognitive-science interests and perspectives, but we believe they need to be answered before we can make substantial headway in (a) designing instruction which can simultaneously optimize acquisition, retention and transfer; and (b) predicting the course of retention across the complete range of tasks and learner abilities. There are simply not enough studies, which have emphasized these kinds of questions in the context of *long-term* retention, for any meta-analysis to be appropriate or advisable.

Although this is labeled as an *Approach* section, we have made several substantive digressions about the nature and adequacy of the relevant literature. These have been necessary for two reasons. First, it should help the reader to appreciate why we could not undertake a conventional meta-analysis. Second, it should set the stage for the cognitive-point of view that we will employ heavily at times to examine, critically and intensively, traditional variables influencing LTR, and to suggest that the ways that *cognitive-processing* variables operate may be more important, finer-grain determinants of LTR. We do not know enough about how these traditional, molar-level variables operate at the *process* level, that is, at the level of the individual's information-processing system, and the cognitive-processing *demands* of both the task and the context of learning.

We have taken full advantage of a wealth of information in the cognitive literature which, in our view, is quite germane, although others may think that it is only indirectly or unimportantly related to LTR. That literature, which is crucially concerned with human encoding and storage processes, issues of knowledge-representation, and retrieval structures and processes, is a promising source of important fresh insights and new theory-based interpretations of old data and accepted verities about LTR.

In addition to examining the literature bearing directly on LTR, we carefully reviewed the cognitively-oriented literature and other sources that we thought are conceptually relevant, e.g., the literature on human amnesia. These were selected after thoughtful consideration of the insights and data they offer about information-processing operations relevant to explaining how people transform, retain and retrieve information.

13

Some of these less-centrally-related sources specifically deal with acquisition and immediate retention. Some are reviews or reports of experiments which shed light on the processing aspects of encoding for learning and remembering, even though the work reviewed was not particularly aimed at these outcomes. These sources, in some cases, *become* extremely useful by providing findings from which we can extrapolate to a broader range of learning contents or contexts *as they relate to LTR*. For example, there is a good-size body of literature on instructional strategies which work, typically, by manipulating the materials or the conditions of learning such that the individual is influenced to form more "elaborate" encodings as he is learning. "Elaborate" is a term which can be defined at several levels, but in the broadest, most generally accepted sense, refers to the richness and range of encodings, and is clearly associated with higher levels of retention (Anderson & Reder, 1979; Craik & Tulving, 1975; Eysenck, 1979; Klein & Saltz, 1976). However, although many different ways have been tried to induce varying kinds and degrees of elaboration, none of them can, in turn, reliably produce improved retention across different domains, learning conditions and differing-ability learners.

However, our point here is two-fold: First, the general concept of enriching or elaborating the memory-trace structure, of organizing what is being learned so that it later will become more quickly and accurately retrieved, has been proven to be a powerfully influential determinant of memorability. Secondly, although very few of these instructional-strategy studies involving elaboration have dealt with long-range retention, much less with military-type tasks, the explanatory potential of the *elaboration* construct is great. Even more importantly, by using cognitive theory along with this indirectly-related literature, we can move more quickly towards the very practical end of designing instruction for optimal long-term retention.

Although we have gone to some lengths to explain that a meta-analysis as such is not appropriate for the literature on LTR, we will, nevertheless, try to follow the spirit of the meta-analytic approach. Wherever it does seem suitable and achievable, we will group selected related studies in chart form, and summarize key findings and conclusions, so that the reader can more readily appreciate, within a comparative framework, the nature and approximate magnitude of any effects found for the same important variables. The studies we choose to chart deal directly with LTR. They comprise not only major reviews (represented in Table A-1), but also reports we consider representative of typical paradigms, reports considered seminal for their time, and reports which produced relatively important, strong or clear data, emphasizing studies performed in the real world of the military.

A meta-analysis "should characterize features of the studies and study outcomes in quantitative or semiquantitative ways" (Kulik, Kulik & Cohen, 1980, p. 527). In an attempt to pin some meaningful numbers on the effects of the major variables influencing LTR, we will use a 1-5 range rating scale to capture quantitatively what we believe is the strength of the effect in question as reflected by the data in the report reviewed. Later in this paper, as we discuss all major variables in detail, we will explain the criteria, subjectively weighted by us, for arriving at our rating.

One last but very important point needs to be made about our general approach and philosophy. No reviews can be exhaustive, if only because no two reviewers will necessarily agree on what is relevant. In our intensive reviews of the centrally relevant papers in this field, we noticed, all too often, that many authors do not cite the literature from other different-but-related communities of interest. Nor do they usually take the time and trouble to pull in and try to relate their findings to what they may consider "exotic" literatures.

Although this review makes no pretense at being exhaustive, we have tried to include the latest major findings and prevailing views representing, for example: (a) the spectrum of researchers directly concerned with the practical problem of LTR. These individuals comprise both the military-training community and the public-education community; (b) educational psychologists and other educational researchers whose interests lie in improving instruction; (c) cognitive-psychology researchers whose interest is on how the human-information-processing system operates; (d) cognitive-science and computer-science researchers whose concern is with how knowledge is represented inside the head. The motivating interest here is frequently the desire to design workable artifical-intelligence (AI) systems; and (e) those researchers whose focus in on human memory, whether it be short-term memory (STM) or LTR, episodic, semantic, procedural, verbal, motor, etc. These terms will be explained as they are encountered.

15

V. THEORETICAL UNDERPINNINGS AND CENTRAL ISSUES

Although we will try, in the rest of this paper, to present and discuss all the key issues, problems and variables in some logically organized order, it will be necessary at times to bring up and briefly discuss certain topics out of turn. This will be unavoidable for at least two reasons: (a) the issues are, for the most part, conceptually interconnected, and the major variables may interact in experiments which are factorially designed to reflect such interactions; and (b) we will want to alert the reader, when we first introduce an issue or a commonly found experimental effect, to our alternative or expanded interpretations of them.

A. THEORIES OF MEMORY AND FORGETTING

In order to explain the phenomenon of forgetting, several different theories of why forgetting occurs have been proposed. There is no reason to believe that these may not all be true, and in fact, may operate simultaneously or alone for any memory.

The trace theory posits that there is an organic residual effect, termed a memory *trace*, of all events and sensations that *register* on the individual. A single trace may be a representation of a simple event or stimulus, or it may stand for a complex, multi-layered set of *related* events. These may be related in some intrinsically meaningful way, or merely because they occurred at the same time or in the same context. *Registration* of an event implies that it was perceived (not necessarily consciously) and then encoded (processed or transformed) into some form of memorial representation. The nature and organization of these representations in memory is currently one of the most actively studied areas in cognitive science. AI researchers would like to create "smart," computer-based systems which can store and access data with the flexibility of a human. Cognitive psychologists use the computer to simulate, and thereby study, how people take in, process, store and retrieve information.

Is forgetting caused by some physical decay or weakening of the trace? The role of rehearsal or practice, one view holds, is to strengthen traces and thus make them more resistant to decay. As time passes, "weak" traces deteriorate unless they are made stronger by repetition or use of the trace. One can accept the trace-decay theory without having to accept any particular view about how traces are organized and mentally catalogued. Obviously, to successfully remember something, some selective *retrieval* process has to be posited, i.e., a process which will locate and contact the correct traces. Such access allows the traces to be recalled (brought into current consciousness) or used to perform some action.

The second major theory of why forgetting occurs treats forgetting as a failure to make contact with the appropriate traces. That failure is presumed to be caused by interfering traces which, because of their similarity to the targeted trace, intrude themselves into the retrieval process and are mistaken for the correct trace. (See Conrad, 1967; Keppel & Underwood, 1962; and McGeoch & Irion, 1952). Of course, similarity between two traces, depending upon its nature and extent, can either interfere with memory or facilitate it. In the latter case, we effect positive transfer.

Logically, the number and kind of distinguishing and distinctive properties of a trace should affect its memorability, since the more distinctive the trace is, the less likely it is to be confused with another one. Conrad (1967) has suggested a modification of decay theory: it considers decay as "a loss of discriminative characteristics...and recall as a process involving discrimination of available traces" (p. 49). If Conrad's theory is accepted, it follows that if we can deliberately design instruction to create distinctive traces, these will be less vulnerable to deterioration. It would further follow that we might also be able to insert the "right kind" of distinctiveness into instructional programs for promoting positive transfer.

Conrad's theory, as we will see later, is in line with several related theories popular in both contemporary educational and cognitive psychology. These theories deal in detail with how traces are mentally represented as complex, meaningful, well-articulated network-like structures. These structures serve as the mind's organized filing system. Since they maintain one's store of K&S, and they are arranged to afford maximum understanding and ease of retrieval, we shall refer to these structures as knowledge-representation/retrieval structures (KRRSs). It is our basic contention in this paper, to be

18

developed as we keep presenting and interpreting additional data, that various characteristics of these KRRSs largely determine the probability that any given attempt to remember something or call a skill into play will be successful.

It is important to point out again that most of the literature on learning and retention talks about forgetting as if there are no qualitative changes in memory as a function of the retention interval. If you believe in the trace-decay theory, there is no logical reason to contend that all aspects of the trace, especially if it represents a complex, multi-sensory network of related facts, procedures and rules, must decay at the same rate. If, on the other hand, you hold to the interference theory, then the accessibility of any particular memorial event may change over time because the type, as well as the amount, of interfering material may change.

Those few early studies which dealt with the qualitative aspects of retention focussed on the memory image (McGeoch & Irion, 1952), using introspective reports as well as having subjects try to draw visual figures they had learned. The results of these types of experiments were mixed at best. Introspective protocols generally revealed a context of reported material much of which had no apparent connection with what was learned. In the case of reproduction of the visual material, Kuhlmann (1906), almost 80 years ago, had his subjects draw meaningless visual forms from memory. He found that his learners, after drawing the more difficult forms from visual memory, would resort to recognition to then modify them further. The subjects sometimes used idiosyncratic verbal associations to evoke their imaginal reproductions. McGeoch & Irion (1952), based upon an analysis of a number of these types of investigations, state that the conclusions are so complex as to rest upon the interpretation of each experimenter. "The results of these studies," they assert, "stand as a vigorous warning that the quantitative data which the usual experiments yield do not tell the whole story of retention" (p. 366).

A third theory as to what causes forgetting holds that it is a function of the affective tone of the material. Generally called the Repression theory, it merely states that any anxiety-provoking or unpleasant memories will be less likely to be recalled. Since psycho-therapy has, as one of its primary goals, to have the patient gain access to, and critically examine, his buried unpleasant memories, the repression view of forgetting suggests that memories become unavailable because the retrieval process is blocked, not because of any biochemical decay. Repression theory does not seem to be particularly useful to consider for purposes of this paper. It gets us into problems of non-cognitive factors which undoubtedly operate to affect recall. However, tackling questions relating to affect and motivation are beyond the scope of this paper. We refer the reader to Snow and Farr (in press) and D'Ydewalle and Lens (1981) for recent perspectives on these issues.

Advocates of the pure organic-decay theory of memory do not necessarily have to hold to any particular neurophysiological view as to how and where memories are stored. For the most part, the contemporary, still-in-its relative-infancy view of the neurologic substrate of memory does not conflict with current cognitive views of human knowledge representation and retrieval processes. At any rate, as with the area of non-cognitive factors, reviewing the literature on the biologic bases of memory is beyond the scope of this paper. If emerging biologically-derived data are seen as particularly relevant to points we are making, we will note this.

B. TYPES OF MEMORY

There are a number of different ways of classifying types of memory. At the highest level, and the one that is most relevant to the distinction between knowledge and skills, is the conclusion (Hirsh, 1974), supported by recent neurophysiologically-oriented research (see, for example, Mishkin & Petri, 1984), that there must be at least two categories of memory -- *fact* memory and *skill* memory. Fact memory refers to memory for explicit information, such as names, dates, locations and words. These types of memories are usually learned relatively quickly, recorded along with the context in which they were acquired, and are frequently easy to forget, especially when the information (such as a phone number that's been changed) is no longer wanted.

In contrast, skill memory is concerned with less conscious learning, typically associated, in part at least, with motor behavior, such as riding a bike, touch typing, and playing tennis. These memories do not seem to preserve the actual circumstances of learning, in the sense that an expert golfer doesn't remember all the practice strokes that led to his proficiency. Furthermore, the skill memories are acquired predominantly by doing, i.e., by practice, and are not easy to unlearn if they are learned wrong. One does not recall skill memory as such -- rather, one demonstrates retention of any particular skill by actually performing it. And many skill memories are performed most effectively without any attendant mental associations.

Adams (1983), referring to fact and skill memory as verbal retention and motor retention, voices the hope that they could be lawfully and theoretically described in the same way. But the issue of how memory traces of motor skills are represented still is a major problem. Does one store memory of a movement, of the distance (extent) and location (end point) of the movement as a unitary entity? Adams (1985) says probably not, and claims that the "ways of encoding dimensions of movements and the implications of them for retention" are "empirically and theoretically underdeveloped" (p. 93). However, Adams implies that the chance for a satisfactory explanation of the durability of motor behavior lies within the province of cognitive variables.

All in all, though, in spite of the promise that some researchers feel that the cognitive perspective holds for understanding motor behavior, Adams (1985) points to two of the reviews (Prophet, 1976; Schendel, Shields, & Katz, 1978) [that we characterize in Table A-1] as underscoring the impression that "long-term motor retention is a domain that is empty of productive ideas, where little or no research is being done" (p. 94). When we discuss the relationship of various types of tasks to LTR, we shall have more to say about motor skills.

One more way of classifying memory is worth discussing, because it is generally representative of current cognitively-oriented, categorizing schemes; this particular formulation purports to "improve the fit between facts and theory" (Tulving, 1985). Tulving believes that memory is composed of three interrelated major systems which are organized structures composed of neural substrates and their behavioral and cognitive correlates. To maintain consistency with previous usage, he calls these systems *procedural*, *semantic* and *episodic*. Each one differs in the way it acquires, represents and expresses knowledge, as well as in the kind of conscious awareness that characterizes its operations.

Procedural memory permits the individual to retain learned connections between complex stimulus and response patterns and to respond to one's environment adaptively. It includes semantic memory as its single, specialized subsystem. Semantic memory is able to represent, internally, states of the world that are not perceptually present. This enables the organism to construct "mental models" of the world. It is the accuracy of these mental models, for any domain of knowledge, that in large part determines how well one *understands* that knowledge. The role of understanding in preserving LTR will be discussed later.

Episodic memory, is, in turn, a subset of semantic memory that provides the organism with the additional capability to acquire and store knowledge about personally experienced events. For practical education and training implications, it seems to be the least important. It needs, however, to be included, Tulving (1985) suggests, in any conceptualization of memory which attempts to be comprehensive.

These memory systems, it should be appreciated, are not merely hypothetical constructs. There is evidence, supporting the existence of classificatory schemes of memory, which comes from experiments designed to study the effects of brain lesions or brain stimulation on the performance of two or more tasks of learning or memory. The basic kind of result relevant to distinguishing among different memory systems is one in which the particular brain injury or stimulation influences performance on one task, but not on the other. (For reviews of these types of findings, see Hirsh, 1974; O'Keefe & Nadel, 1978; and Oakley, 1981.)

Why is it important to try to identify and contrast different kinds of memory systems? For one thing, when any particular activity is being directed by something in memory, the characteristics of the actual performance are reflections of the kind or system of memory. The *specificity* and *organizational "complexity"* of the way that the stored knowledge is represented in memory will strongly influence how well that information will be retained, used for its intended purpose, and be able successfully to facilitate (i.e., positively transfer to) the learning of extra-domain knowledge.

"It is inappropriate to talk about discrete memory traces" (Tulving, 1985, p. 388), where procedural memory is concerned. This kind of memory, however, is prescriptive: it contains a stored action plan, analogous to a computer program which determines how well any given routine or subroutine is "run off." Procedural memory, like the computer program, doesn't need information about the past to serve its purpose. The price that the human pays for having his memories "compiled" into the format of procedural memory is inflexibility: "Only direct expression is possible...; overt responding according to a relatively rigid format determined at the time of learning is obligatory" (Tulving, 1985, p. 388).

22

In contrast, semantic memory is not compiled. Its representations describe the world without dictating any particular action. This kind of memory is thus less restrictive, and can manifest itself under *conditions* quite different from those found in original learning, and in *performance* which is also dissimilar to that involved in the original learning process. The implications for transfer of training of this distinction should be reasonably evident.

VI. RELATIONSHIP BETWEEN ACQUISITION AND RETENTION

A. LEARNING MASTERY AND OVERLEARNING

Although this paper is devoted to the retention phase of learning and memory, we can not meaningfully separate retention from acquisition. At the risk of stating the rather obvious, we all realize that a piece of knowledge or skill has to be acquired before it can be retained and retrieved. On the other hand, we can only determine whether a person has successfully learned something by having him demonstrate its retention, even if that retention endures for only a very short time. Retention, i.e., the outcome of successful learning, *seems* to be a straightforward concept, one that we typically measure by having the learner recognize, recall, repeat or reproduce what he has acquired.

However, the relationship between acquisition and retention is far from simple. At what point in the learning stage do we decide that acquisition is successful or complete? Part of the answer here is that the criterion for successful learning (frequently called *mastery*) in any given case is arbitrary. In the classroom setting, an examination of some sort is used to document successful learning, and all those people who pass the test (for example, getting between 65% and 100% of the questions correct) are deemed to have learned well enough to apply that knowledge to the real world, or to take the next module or course moving them on to more advanced material.

In the experimental laboratory setting, or in the teaching of "hands-on" procedural skills to military personnel, the mastery criterion frequently is expressed in terms of how many times the learner can successively perform the entire [typically sequential] task without error. Quite often, the individual is deemed to have mastered his material if he manages to execute a single, fully successful trial. In such a case, if we measure the performance of the person *after* his first perfect trial, we are measuring his retention of the task. But, for the same task and a different learner, we might just as well have decided not to consider the task as "mastered" until he had repeated it perfectly three times in a row.

25

The potential confusion and ambiguity created in this case by nothing more than two arbitrarily different, operational definitions of a mastery criterion need to be appreciated. If these two different hypothetical learners were each subjects in a different experiment that was examining, say, the effect of a particular instructional strategy on LTR, we might well get opposite results. For example, let's suppose experiment #1, using a single, errorless trial as the mastery criterion, shows that the instructional strategy has no effect on the amount of material retained after a 4-week period. The second experiment, using a criterion of three errorless trials, reveals that the *same* instructional variable has the statistically significant effect of *increasing* the relative amount of material retained after the same 4-week nonuse interval.

The conflicting results obtained by these two hypothetical findings could easily be attributable to their different mastery criteria. As we will discuss later, the *degree* or *amount* of original learning is a powerful influence on how much is retained, and for how long; that is, the degree, or level of difficulty of the mastery criterion must be taken into account in interpreting any studies relating acquisition variables to retention. In the made-up example just given, it is quite likely that the extra two errorless trials, considered to be merely part of the acquisition phase, produced enough "extra" learning (what we have been calling "overlearning") to be responsible for the significant improved-retention effect.

The confusion frequently created by not adequately, precisely and explicitly considering the arbitrary nature and definition of a mastery criterion is reinforced by Lane's (in press) assertion that group learning curves may, in part, not accurately represent individual curves because of the problem in defining mastery. Lane reported that virtually no data were available on individual performance which involved a realistic criterion level at which training can be terminated.

B. THE "STRENGTH" OF RETENTION

In general, it seems logical that the more *strongly* one learns something, the more resistant that material or skill ought to be to forgetting. The seminal issue, *both* practically and theoretically, can be posed in terms of what it means for a given trace network (what we've termed a KRRS) or set of associations to be "stronger" than another. In a purely pragmatic sense, if the probability that a given cue c will elicit learned response x is greater than that it will elicit learned response y, we can say that the strength of the association (or memory trace, if you will) between c and x is greater than that between c and y.

Having said this, we have said nothing which guides us heuristically in the sense of revealing how to design instruction that produces the *strongest* memories. What does this concept of associative or memory strength really mean? Does it apply in a brute-force sense, telling us that the more you practice, that the longer you drill and repeat, the more strongly embedded will be the trace? The simplest analogy here is to think that the strength of a trace is like hammering in a nail. Does every learning trial or repetition pound in the trace a little deeper each time?

On the other hand, does strengthening a memory mean that we change its KRRS so that its internal organization and relationship to other KRRSs are modified to make successful retrieval more likely? Mandler (1968), for example, suggested that "the strengthening of an associative structure means that the organism learns more efficient search paths among the members of that structure" (p. 115). We suggested earlier in this paper that certain qualitative characteristics of the KRRS will strongly influence its memorability. These attributes, which will be discussed later, are pointers to how complexly organized and richly cross-referenced are the components.

The issue of what makes for a "strong" (durable and accessible) memory is at the theoretical heart of any set of prescriptions that can be promulgated to promote LTR. We contend that every variable that has been empirically identified as affecting the rate or extent of decay might profitably be examined from the following points of view: (a) How does the variable affect the specific KRRSs in which the to-be-retrieved material is embedded? and (b) How does the variable affect the "search path" which must be traversed to access the relevant KRRSs, and then, additionally, contact exactly the specific targeted trace component within? These questions are obviously fundamental if one holds the view that forgetting is primarily a failure to retrieve potentially accessible traces. Given that viewpoint, it follows that the best course of action lies in developing instructional material and techniques to make the traces of our learning products more prominent, more discriminable, more locatable -- in short, more memorable.

Given the belief that sheer repetition and amount of effort exerted during learning can "strengthen" a trace network so that it is more resistant to decay, the logical prescription for retarding forgetting is to increase repetitions, drill and practice, and/or to demand a high degree of overlearning.

The *prevailing* viewpoint about the main cause of forgetting is one of retrieval failure (Stern, 1981; Wood, 1983). This could be a result of interference by competing responses, or the result of a target trace that is not mentally discriminable enough to be readily located and identified. This is not to say that those who hold to the interference belief deny any time-dependent trace decay. Rather, they tend to hold that the nature of the retrieval process and knowledge structures are more potent variables to be manipulated.

Probably the first major cognitive theory that tried to explain memory in terms of human information processing was that using the "levels of processing" framework (Craik & Lockhart, 1972). They formulated this approach in an attempt to explain different retention characteristics of three posited levels of human-memory storage: sensory stores, short-term store (STS), and long-term store (LTS).

Stimuli can enter the sensory store even though they do not "register," in other words, even when the individual is not paying any attention to the source. This sensory store is, therefore, said to be *pre-attentive* (Neisser, 1976). If the person *attends* to the material in his sensory store, he is effectively reading it out (i.e., registering it), and thereby transferring it to STS. In this latter register, verbal items, for example, are coded into phonemes or into auditory-verbal-linguistic terms. The loss rate of information in STS is on the order of 5 to 20 seconds, as compared to the 1/4 to 2-seconds decay rate of the sensory store. STS has a limited capacity: its information is lost by some form of decay or by being displaced by new entering information. In contrast, LTS has no known capacity limit, and usually has its verbal (roughly equatable with propositional or factual) material coded in terms of semantic features (Craik & Lockhart, 1972).

We have taken the time to explain these hypothesized memory registers because the *processing* of information is what moves raw data along so that it is encoded and transferred to long-term memory. We contend that the depth and kind of processing or coding play a vital role in determining resistance to forgetting. We will consider in detail all those factors, materials and conditions of learning which can affect the depth and extent of the processing so as to make the coded material more accessible to memory, and less subject to interference (negative transfer). Obviously, the nature and complexity of the material or skill to be learned, and one's expectations of how and when he will be called upon to demonstrate his proficiency will determine, in large part, how carefully and precisely the information is encoded. But the instructional designer should be able, we maintain, to employ instructional strategies that can, at least in part, overcome the burden of material or skills that are difficult to learn and remember. And those strategies can be most effective by attacking the problem of memory loss at its source, the trace complex we have labeled the KRRS.

C. ROLE OF TIME

Most instructional strategies are aimed at improving the particular learning outcome of an acquisition stage, i.e., the mastery of some material or skill. If these strategies consider the two additional learning outcomes of retention and transfer at all, they are usually only secondary considerations. The instructor or instructional designer, after all, wants to get as many students to reach the mastery criterion, within the available time, as possible. Sometimes, but not often, the *time* taken to reach the criterion is itself part of the criterion. This is usually the case when one is being trained for a task or job for which time pressure is inherent, for example, emergency procedures or air-traffic control.

Most real-life tasks are not speeded, in the sense that, if one fails to perform them successfully within a given time period, one has failed the task. There is evidence that *time to learn* is a significantly stronger correlate (e.g., for 4th to 6th graders studying math computation, math concepts, vocabulary, reading comprehension, reading for facts and spelling) of school achievement than is a group-administered IQ test (Gettlinger & White, 1979). The issue of time to learn as a mastery criterion and as a variable subject to individual differences will be taken up shortly.

From a theoretical vantage point, time is important because a longer duration allows more opportunities for whatever operation is going on. During the learning phase, allowing the trainee more time gives him more chance for practice, for encoding the material so that it is adequately understood and integrated into his existing memorial data base. In other words, more learning time allows for more *processing time*; the latter allows for more *processing depth* and *elaboration*, and for a greater variety of learning strategies to be invoked and successfully employed by the learner.

Time, of course, is also manipulated, in some sense, when we vary the scheduling or spacing of learning trials or practice occasions. The effect of massed versus distributed practice during training has been reviewed by Lane (in press) as a variable influencing the products of acquisition. In this connection, Bahrick (1979) makes a cogent observation about how we learn much of the day-to-day, real-life information that is usually retained for a lifetime. Most of this "semipermanent knowledge," as he labels it, is picked up over extended time periods during which actual practice is limited to relatively short sessions spaced at differing intervals. Examples that Bahrick gives are knowledge learned in formal settings, such as school courses; learning how to play games such as chess or bridge; and learning the names and faces of the people we meet and the locations and arrangements of streets and buildings we frequent. Practice sessions may or may not be clearly delineated but, typically, time intervals of varying lengths separate practice sessions. The point is that, without repeated, prolonged exposure to the same information during a single session, only a small amount of the material learned during the initial exposure remains permanently in memory. A substantial part, therefore of what we learn on one exposure may be forgotten until the next exposure provides a relearning opportunity. "One can, therefore, conceive of the total acquisition process as a cycle of information with diminishing amounts of information lost during the intervals between exposures until the information becomes part of permanent knowledge retrievable without further learning" (Bahrick, 1979, pp. 297-298).

The argument made by Bahrick is particularly relevant not only to the variable of time, but also to the relationship between acquisition and forgetting. Melton (1963) highlighted this, in a major theoretical article, arguing that learning, even within a single session composed of many trials, represents the *cumulative* effects of *alternating* cycles of learning and forgetting. In spite of this relationship, contends Bahrick (1979), memory research has not dealt directly with these *repeated* cycles which characterize the way we learn most of life's essentially permanent K&S. He decries most laboratory studies of LTM as not being ecologically valid, a point that Neisser (1976) echoed by asking for a "...commitment to the study of variables that are ecologically important rather than those that are easily manageable" (p. 7).

We have previously suggested that whether a practice trial is considered to occur during acquisition or after acquisition can depend on a (frequently) arbitrary definition of the mastery criterion used to index the end of acquisition. The Bahrick (1979) and Melton (1963) view just expressed maintains that the *transition* from the acquisition to the retention phase is continuous, rather than discrete, and is probably a function of the time durations between *reacquisition* sessions. In a real sense, each item learned is maintained in memory, ready for use immediately after it's been acquired, but is lost again and must be reacquired if the following attempt at retrieval is delayed too long. Bahrick (1979) thus reaches the logical conclusion that the distinction between learning and retention phases "...is meaningful only in relation to particular intervals between successive exposures during acquisition, and to intervals between retrieval attempts during the maintenance phase" (p. 299).

D.   THE CURVE OF RETENTION

The passage of time after acquisition, accompanied by nonuse of the learned K or S, leads to a decay curve which is frequently called a curve of retention. Amount of retention is typically plotted against time elapsed since original learning. This retention curve, which Ebbinghaus (1885/1913) first plotted from his experiments with nonsense syllables, is usually negatively accelerated: the curve falls most quickly during the time immediately following acquisition, and declines more and more slowly over time. McGeoch and Irion (1952) claim that the general shape of the decay curve, even though initially derived from and representative of nonsense materials, also holds for the verbatim memory of meaningful material, over a wide range of experimental conditions. However, there is an overall higher retention rate for the meaningful material.

In comparing the Ebbinghaus curve with recall of English words and the recall of factual prose, McGeoch and Irion (1952) suggest that, as the meaningfulness of the material increases, the rate of forgetting slows down, and the lower asymptote of the retention curve appears to rise. These authors caution that this conclusion applies to verbal learning only; they also offer a more sweeping, more important cautionary note: that the "...curve of retention...reflects a constancy attitude toward the phenomena of retention and can be exceedingly misleading, since relationships other than the one depicted can be found" (p. 355).

We will consider some of these other "relationships" later when we discuss, for example, memory for prose and text. In addition, we will examine the proposition that the varied component parts that constitute a meaningful, complex task decay at different rates during nonuse intervals. And we will discuss the hotly contested (Slamecka & McElree, 1983; Loftus, 1985) issue of how the level of original learning affects the rate of forgetting.

E. MEASURES OF RETENTION

Anyone who has ever taken a multiple-choice test, a fill-in-the-blank-space completion test, or an essay test knows that these tests all seem to tap one's relevant knowledge differently. We refer, for example, to the fact that we can frequently *recognize* the correct answer, but not produce it by free *recall*.

The differences between these two common measures of retention are reflected in other ways. A number of investigators have found that the extent of organization (for example, comparing a list of conceptually related words with a list of unrelated words) affected recall more than recognition (Wood, 1983). If we have to recall information, rather than to recognize it, then its organization, or the use of a strategy to associate related items, is much more influential (Kintsch, 1968, 1970).

When we prepare ourselves for an essay test, we are more likely to focus on such aspects as how the information is organized, on the reasons for and against particular theories, or on the causes of events. On the other hand, for multiple-choice tests, we generally stress factual knowledge -- dates, places, names, etc. Interestingly, if individuals *expect* a recognition test, they do better on it than if they expect a recall test and instead receive the recognition test (Carey & Lockhart, 1973).

In many instances an individual's ability to recognize an event seems unrelated to his ability to recall the event. For example, Tulving and Weisman (1975) found that, under some circumstances, people were not much better at recognizing words that they were able to recall than they were at overall recognition. They were given a recall test on a list of words, followed by a recognition test. If recall and recognition are related, recognition performance should be better for words that were recalled than for the other words. Under some circumstances there is little relation, suggesting that recall and recognition *can* sometimes be independent processes (see also Flexser & Tulving, 1978). The relation between recall and recognition can be viewed in terms of differential coding: we code attributes or features of events, and certain codes are more suitable for some kinds of retention tests than for others.

The typical curve of retention described earlier is a measure of how long it takes a person to *relearn* the material [to the same mastery criterion as that of original learning (OL)] as compared to how long it took for the OL to occur. In many of the experimental laboratory studies, recognition or free recall have been used, in addition to the relearning techniques, to measure retention. There are a number of other measures of retention which can be used. We already referred to the qualitative changes in nonsense figures which were measured by Kuhlmann (1906); he had his experimental subjects reproduce them by drawing what they remembered.

Luh (1922), in his experiments on the effects of the overlearning of nonsense syllables on retention, systematically compared five different measures: recognition, reconstruction (of the original order of the list), written reproduction, recall by anticipation, and relearning. Although all the retention curves were negatively accelerated, they had different slopes (rates of decline). None of the curves crossed except for that of relearning, which intersected those for written reproduction and reconstruction.

F. RELEARNING

Relearning deserves special attention in a discussion about retention because it has an unusual characteristic: it is comprised of two factors. The very first trial or attempt to relearn involves the *same* procedure as that used in OL, and can therefore be scored as a retention measure in its own right. Because the person then continues with additional learning trials until he regains his initial mastery level, we can compute a savings score. Logically the two constituent factors are inversely related -- the more that one recalls in his first relearning trial, the fewer should be the number of additional trials to relearn. However, as we shall see later, in many actual studies, including some real-world ones, there appears to be no definable or consistent relationship between the relearning (savings) score and the first-trial recall measure. An individual might, for example, manifest very poor retention in his first relearning trial, yet proceed to show a very high savings score. This is not at all far-fetched. For example, based on an extensive historical review, Adams

(1985) concludes: "Forgetting of procedural responses can be complete in about a year, although relearning is rapid" (p. 53).

In addition to the confused relationship between amount retained and the savings score of relearning, the latter apparently differs considerably across different tasks. For example, Ammons et al. (1958), examined the relearning of a continuous-control motor task which had been practiced, in OL, for 8 hours. After 6 months of nonuse, the subjects relearned the task within 13-14 minutes. However, extrapolation of a 15-step procedural task that had been learned over 30 practice trials led to the conclusion that at least 15 trials would be needed to regain the original mastery level after a 6-month interval of nonuse (Gagne, in press). When we compare these two tasks in savings-score terms, the motor-skill-retention index is 97%, while the procedural skill yields only a 50% savings.

From the existing evidence about relearning, it appears that, for any particular skilled performance, we cannot predict its rate of relearning as a function of its OL. Gagne (in press) concludes that "the relation between amount recalled and amount of relearning required is not known" (p. 21).

There are *some* consistent data in the area of relearning that do permit some useful conclusions to be made where motor skills are concerned. Schendel, Shields and Katz (1978) present evidence that (a) the time to retrain is generally consistently less than 50% of the original learning time; (b) the "retraining time is much longer for longer retention intervals, more difficult tasks, and for procedural tasks rather than continuous tasks" (p. 16).

The implications of the lack of correspondence between retention measured by recall and by relearning are considerable. For practical purposes, especially with respect to military training, we're interested in how severely a K or S has decayed so that we can determine if the deterioration has progressed far enough to degrade readiness. Given such an unacceptable amount of decay, we then need to know how long it will take, and at what resource cost, to bring personnel proficiency back up to an acceptable level. Thus, what the training manager needs to know is when and how much refresher-training is necessary, and what the concomitant resource requirements are.

G.   RECALL VS. RECOGNITION

In everyday life, the relative roles of recognition and recall interact constantly. Events and information that are not available to recall can, given the appropriate cuing, suddenly pop into awareness. Consider the following example of a typical way in which apparently "lost" memories are reactivated. You may have once followed a set of explicit directions for driving to a particular restaurant in a city you had never visited before. You made no attempt to commit the route to memory, and several years later, when you visit the city for a second time, you decide you would like to dine in the same restaurant. You try to remember its name or location, but all you can vaguely recall is that it specialized in seafood, was at least a 15-minute trip from your hotel (the same one you're staying at this second time around), and you think it had a nautical-sounding name. You pass on this sparse set of dim memories to the hotel clerk, and ask him if he can identify the restaurant. He immediately says: "That sounds like Captain Mike's restaurant, right off the Grandview exit of Interstate 86. It has a big yellow sign with a picture of a bearded sea captain on it." You immediately say: "That's the place. I remember that sign, *now that you reminded me.*"

You can't recall a single detail about how to get to the restaurant, so you get directions from the clerk. Rather than draw a map, he gives you *procedural* directions. ["Turn right out of the hotel parking lot, proceed about 1/4 mile to Walnut Street (just past the firehouse); go left on Walnut for about a mile. Just after you pass the parking lot for Randolph's Department Store, turn left and it'll take you to the on-ramp for Interstate 186..."].

As you listen to these directions, you say to yourself: "Oh sure, now I remember that store -- when I first saw it I was surprised that a town this small would have such a large store." And, as you follow the directions, you stop at a traffic light alongside of a brightly-lit professional office building with a list of physicians' and dentists' names posted on an easily visible sign. Suddenly, another memory you couldn't possibly dredge up from free recall comes flooding into your mind. You remember passing this place three years ago because you mentally noted then that one of the dentist's surnames, an uncommon name, was the same as that of your own dentist, and you wondered if they were related.

35

What we've illustrated by this sample scenario is just how differentially sensitive are the mechanisms of free recall and recognition that can manifest themselves in our day-to-day world. When certain retrieval cues are provided, especially in the same general context as when the initial information was first acquired, trace contact is made and recognition memory results.

The scenario just described also illustrates how apparently extraneous, irrelevant associations made during the original experience became part and parcel of the KRRS laid down at the time. In spite of the fact that you had *no intention* of remembering the restaurant or how to get there, parts of that initial experience became memorially associated with your previously acquired, relatively permanent knowledge base. For example, the association between the dentist's name on the sign you noticed for perhaps 10 seconds several years before became linked with a KRRS of episodic memory about your own dentist. And any associative linkage can serve as a cue or trigger to activate part or all of the KRRSs to which it belongs. We use the plural form of KRRS here deliberately, to make the point that your dentist's name may be part of multiple KRRSs, representing different kinds of memory. For example, in addition to being part of the episodic KRRS of being one's personal dentist, his name is probably also part of a procedural KRRS of how to get to his office from your home or workplace.

H. CODING FOR RETENTION

We have seen, in the last section on Measures of Retention, that different ways of assessing retention can yield different results, and that how we process or code what we are learning may favor one particular retention technique over another. In an intentional-learning situation, where individuals know from the start how they will be expected to demonstrate that they have achieved mastery, they will tend to code the material to meet the requirements of the retention test. But even when the material to be learned does not seem to lend itself to any kind of coding -- when it is meaningless, unfamiliar, hard to image and lacking structure, subjects can, given sufficient processing time and effort, impose enough organization and meaning so as to make the material learnable and retainable.

For example, suppose that a psychology laboratory experiment calls for learning three lists of paired nonsense syllables of very low associative value. These syllables are learned, for each list, by having the subjects briefly view the left-side member of each pairing alone, and then anticipate its right-side associate. All that would seem to be acquired in this situation is an arbitrary connection of two items, each consisting of meaningless, unpronounceable groups of letters. Yet, even in this seemingly barren learning environment, most subjects not only eventually master this very difficult learning task, but also form a surprising number of ancillary associations.

Evidence for this assertion stems from the fact that the individual, upon reaching mastery, can successfully answer the following types of questions:

(a) Given any member of a pair, he can supply the other member;

(b) Given any two members of different pairs, he can state whether they came for the same list;

(c) After all 3 lists are mastered, given any member of a pair from any list, he can successfully state which list it appeared in by referring to the temporal ordering of the list;

(d) Asked to recall as many pairs or members of pairs from a given list (identified by the experimenter as the first, second or third list), he can demonstrate significant retention of pairs and knowledge of their list membership;

(e) Given another list of nonsense-syllable members or pairs, some of which came from one of the lists learned, and some of which were not ever shown to him, the subject can correctly discriminate "old" from "new" items.

In addition to all these "extra" associations that the subjects frequently form -- which derive completely from within the material presented and the learning context -- many subjects also reveal definite associations they created between the meaningless syllables and materials, events and episodes in their existing store of knowledge (referred to, frequently, as *world knowledge*). To illustrate: a subject might help himself remember that "kaj-lyn" was a pair by coding it into "caged lion," demonstrating a fairly standard kind of mnemonic assist that many people provide for themselves in an attempt to relate new material to world knowledge.

We can extract a lesson from this extreme example of the use of active processing strategies to learn unusually difficult material. It follows, at least in theory, that we should be able to improve learning and retention dramatically if we start out with already meaningful, well-organized items of information which are taught by instructional strategies designed to further promote distinctive, discriminable and traversable search-and-retrieval pathways between the percept/cue and the KRRS, as well as within and among KRRSs. This assertion is especially important if one accepts the prevailing view that forgetting is predominantly a retrieval-process failure.

I. RECALL AND RECOGNITION IN TERMS OF RETRIEVAL

Given the importance of the retrieval operation, we will now turn to considering how the phenomena of recognition and recall inform us about the nature of retrieval and point clearly, we believe, to the cognitive, strategic nature of the process.

All successful remembering, no matter how measured, requires successful retrieval in response to some sort of cue, whether internally generated or externally provided. In the case of recognition failure, the cue is not defined well enough, or its target trace is so obscured by similar interfering traces, that the necessary contact between percept and trace is not made. However, although recognition does not occur in the sense of successful identification or matching, what may result is a sense of familiarity -- the realization that one has encountered this cue before, but just cannot conjure up any particulars.

One information-processing type of interpretation of this is that we have made contact with the KRRS which *contains* the target trace, but can't penetrate any further because of blockage or interference. In some analogical sense, the "flashlight" illuminating one's model of search is not bright enough, nor the trace discriminable enough, for recognition to take place.

In recall, you have a more difficult memory demand. You must take the information given to you and deduce, based on the nature and requirements of the recall test, conditions and context, what are the relevant cues or descriptors needed to *construct* a memory-search *plan*. For example, refer to the task, described above, of learning several lists of nonsense syllables. By the free-recall method, one might require the learner to recite or write down as many members of the second list, in any order, as he could remember. To perform this successfully, the only obvious trace that the subject must have laid down is the one created by the temporal ordering of the lists, since the different lists learned were not identified in any way. (See Underwood, 1977, for an intensive analysis of the possible processes behind temporal memory coding.)

Yet, in spite of the fact that this temporal-ordering trace is the only operative one, subjects are easily capable of succesfully performing this list-membership identification task. And they can do this even though they had no idea, while they were learning the lists, that identity and order were relevant properties to attend to.

We have gone into a somewhat extended discussion of the role of the different types of retention-measuring techniques because they are intimately linked with the retrieval process. And an understanding of this process depends crucially on the relationshjip between the cue and the KRRS.

Our conception of trying to remember something is as follows: You search your long-term memory store in order to locate a target item with a particular relationship to the memory-task cue. The relationship can be one of semantic similarity, of physical-feature similarity, of cause and effect, of membership in the same category, etc. In order to perform this memory search, you transform the cue into a *model of search*, based on all the information you have about the target item.

The model of search consists of a description of some element or aspect or fragment of the item. How complete or how "rich" that description is determines the ease of access or probability of locating the target information. The model of search is used to recover a *new* piece of information about the sought-for item, which is added to what is already known. A more extensive description is then formed, and used to retrieve still more information. This cycle continues until the specific target information can be contacted in its entirety. Successful retrieval is thereby accomplished.

Let's consider an example of how this memory-search process might work for LTR. Suppose you are trying to remember the names of as many classmates as you can from your senior year at high school 10 years earlier. Your model of search is focussed on those KRRSs which have something to do with a host of companion networks which might bear labels like "people I once knew," or more specifically, "people I once knew 10 to 15 years ago when I was in high school," or even more narrowly, "people I knew 10 years ago who were members of my senior class." You may or may not have a KRRS for this last target category of search. If you do, your model of search penetrates (accesses) it, and you read out the contents.

If you lack the exactly appropriate KRRS, you enter one or more *related* KRRSs and try to extract the relevant information by mentally trying out a variety of possible, indirect associations. For example, you may focus on the KRRS representing who attended your high school prom. From that, you can read out names which you might otherwise never have been able to access.

Williams and Hollan (1981) conducted an intensive series of protocol analyses of subjects thinking aloud while trying to recall the names of their high school classmates of from 4 to 19 years before. Even after ten hours of effort, several of their subjects were still dredging up new, correct names.

What Williams concluded from this study is that retrieval is largely *both* a problem-solving activity and a reconstructive process. These combined operations are characterized by the clear presence of different search *strategies*, as well as individual differences in the depth and duration of how these strategies are applied.

J. RECAPITULATION: IMPLICATIONS OF THE FORGETTING PROCESS

We have, up to this point, focussed on giving the reader a fairly comprehensive, stage-setting perspective on such factors as: the nature, kinds and causes of forgetting; ways of classifying memory by types; and the importance of the way knowledge is represented and retrieved. Perhaps, most importantly, our hidden agenda have been to impart an appreciation of how tangled a web is memory, and how essential to understanding memory are the concepts of the strength and quality of the processing operations performed.

In order to provide the necessary background data to the reader, we have occasionally digressed to expand on points that we felt were important to address or highlight at the time. Shortly, in the next major section, we will present and discuss empirical findings and conclusions that characterize the major variables influencing LTR. As an augmented perspective from which to view these to-be-presented data and the traditional interpretatons made about them, we now briefly integrate and recapitulate some salient points we have put forth. Our purpose is to build on them and to draw what we believe are the most plausible inferences for improved training and LTR. The reader is encouraged to consider the mechanisms and constructs we suggest as alternative logical, explanatory frameworks for the findings and conclusions to be discussed in the sections to follow.

We previously discussed the causes of memory loss, and asserted that retrieval failure was the prevailing belief to account for it. We also emphasized that the other main proposed mechanism, that of organic-trace decay, *could* operate side by side with the retrieval inadequacy.

Retrieval failure itself can operate in several different ways. Again, none of these ways is antithetical to any other. Failure to retrieve implies failure to access the relevant trace. That lack of contact might occur for the following reasons:

(a) Interference among the KRRSs or within a KRRS so that the sought-for component trace is not distinguishable enough from similar or related traces to be identified. Discriminability or similarity can be physical, conceptual, semantic, categorical, etc.

(b) If the traces were laid down in some negatively emotional or traumatic context, some kind of mental barrier might be placed around the involved KRRSs. The result is that attempts at retrieval may fail because the model of search cannot penetrate an encapsulated, "fenced-off" KRRS.

(c) The components of a KRRS may be tightly packed together, compiled (in the case of procedural memory) into chunks such that their individual identity may be obscured. This may be what happens with very well overlearned perceptual-motor skills such as playing a piano or piloting an aircraft. It may also be characteristic of the way that the knowledge of a subject-matter (domain) expert, such as a physicist, is represented. Such an expert sometimes cannot readily recall certain individual details that he learned early in the process of becoming an expert.

(d) Depending on the specificity of the cue or the question asked, the model of search that the learner creates may not carry enough information to locate any relevant KRRSs. And, in turn, the relevant KRRSs and their constituent traces may not be strongly discriminable enough to be easily locatable. How readily they can be found, as we have

41

proposed earlier, is a function of how strongly, deeply and elaborately the KRRS is established.

If we accept physical trace decay as a significant source of forgetting, it would seem logical that the stronger one "hammers in" the trace, the more impervious it would be to time-dependent decay.

If retrieval failure is the dominant cause of forgetting, we might plausibly posit that the following kinds of steps be taken. (These are keyed to the (a)-(d) reasons suggested above for why successful retrieval might not occur.)

(a) Interference due to competing traces, which are confused with the correct traces, can be reduced, as a cause of memory failure, by having the trainee deliberately learn fine discriminations, and/or by requiring him to overcome severe interference during the acquisition phase. Battig (1972, 1978) and Shea and Morgan (1979), for example, have shown that increased contextual interference during verbal learning, rule learning and motor learning results in significantly improved retention and transfer. Battig (1978) asserts that, in order to resist contextual interference, subjects employ a number of different processing strategies that result in more elaborate and distinctive processing of the material being learned. This special processing both promotes LTM and decreases the dependence of memory on the reinstatement of the original context. (Positive transfer is an additional benefit that accrues because the processing strategies induced help the individual learn other material.)

(b) To prevent negative affect such as anxiety from repressing memories, one can make learning less stressful, more enjoyable (in the sense of more game-like), and more individualized to the trainee's attitudes, values and ability level. Although not particularly germane to civilian or military training, the process of successful psychotherapy to uncover repressed memories, if understood, might well shed important light on how memory is represented and accessed.

(c) The problem of compiled information is not really a practical problem for our purposes. It is probably a very useful area to investigate further if one's interest lies in the nature of knowledge representation in the expert (see, for example, Chi, Glaser & Farr, in press), or in the kind of overlearning represented by automaticity in skilled performance (Shiffrin & Schneider, 1977; Schneider, Dumais & Shiffrin, 1984).

42

(d) Memory search involves a cue of some sort, as well as a KRRS that the cue must, in some fashion, access and activate. This simply-stated relationship probably underlies the basic and most powerful principle for designing instruction to maximize retention: The organization of the K&S to be learned, and the conditions of learning should be such as to promote the formation of richly elaborated KRRSs. The "stronger" and more discriminable a KRRS is, the more likely it is to be accessed by a "weak," partial or poorly aimed model of search (Williams and Hollan, 1981).

VII. MAJOR VARIABLES AFFECTING LONG-TERM RETENTION

In this section, we characterize the nature and impact of the major variables shown to have influenced LTR. These variables are listed, and their effects summarized, in Tables A-2 through A-7. They comprise (a) the degree of original learning, which is frequently stated in terms of having reached a pre-set criterion of mastery; (b) the characteristics of the learning task, e.g., the type of task and its complexity; (c) the instructional strategies that usually determine the conditions of learning; (d) the length of the retention interval (but it sometimes includes activities, e.g., mental rehearsal, that some learners might engage in *during* this period); (e) the method used to test the extent of retention; and (f) individual differences among trainee usually ability differences as indexed by some standardized test such as the Armed Services Vocational Aptitude Battery (ASVAB).

The data in Tables A-2 through A-7 summarize, for each of these variables, the conclusions reached by 7 key reviews spanning the 1961-1983 time period. These particular reviews were selected because they represent either the most recent and relatively comprehensive surveys whose focus is on *long*-term retention, or reviews of LTR emphasizing selected domains such as flight skills or common enlisted military tasks. There is one other review (E. Gagne, 1978) that deals with LTR of verbal skills within the relatively narrow confines of prose learning. We present a separate table (Table C-1) summarizing her findings because the variables she found most germane were peculiar to reading and remembering the contents of prose passages. More about the Gagne study later.

We prepared Table A-1 to characterize each of the 7 reviews which we use as the source of Tables A-2 through A-7. Our purpose was to allow the reader to obtain a narratively-drawn, capsule comparison of their scope, comprehensiveness, main emphases, and the issues they identify as most important. In the Scope section of this report, we briefly noted the different objectives of these reviews. One strong, overall impression that we hope that Table A-1 conveys is a point we have emphasized earlier:

there seems to be little basic disagreement over what is the general empirical effect of the identified variables on LTR. However, as we also alluded to earlier, there are *fundamental* problems, generally not confronted by these reviews, such as adequate definitions of concepts (e.g., overlearning) and of common metrics (e.g., for retention) that pervade the field and cast real doubt on the apparent agreement.

Annett (1979) recognizes these limitations and adds that, in spite of this, most researchers have uncomplainingly accepted, apparently at face value, broad empirical generalizations about the influence of major variables on *gross* performance measures. As we note in our summary (in Table A-1) of Annett's review, he is cognitively oriented, and tries to reinterpret current views in light of this orientation. We strongly endorse his assertion that a crucial question has been scarcely addressed by most review articles, namely, *what* exactly is forgotten when complex, skilled performance decays over time. However, his question does not explicitly confront the equally important and related issue we have already stressed several times: what has happened, and why, to trace *availability* in response to any specified cue, after varying periods of nonuse?

We will now discuss, in turn, each one of the variables identified in Tables A-2 through A-7. Our concern will not be to restate what the tables already present: the cross-checked and mostly consensual conclusions from these seven reviews, which can be examined in detail by any interested reader. Rather, we will attempt to highlight the *theoretical* implications of the findings and, where applicable, reinterpret them and point out limitations and inconsistencies. In the later sections of this report, we will discuss the *practical* implications of our theoretical formulation in terms of prescriptions for instructional design and predictions of retention loss based on training conditions, training-achievement data, task complexity and the cognitive-demand burden.

The meaning of the columns labeled "Judged Strength of Effect" in Tables A-2 through A-7 needs to be clarified before we proceed to discuss the variables identified. The "effect" referred to is, of course, the effect on the course of forgetting or skill decay. The "strength of effect" is our *judgment* of how clearly, strongly and consistently the variable affects retention in a predictable way. We used no explicit formula to arrive at the strength rating. Instead, we subjectively judged the design of the experiments which provided the data for the conclusions, the sample sizes, the statistical analyses, the consistency and pattern of the effect across different kinds of tasks, learning conditions, ability factors, populations, and experimenters.

The strongest effect received a 5, the weakest a zero. An example of the latter is seen in Table A-4, for the instructional variable of massed vs. distributed learning. We note there, in the second column (for Annett's variable A) that the literature he reviewed shows "no clear superiority." In other cases, we have noted that no effect was found, or inserted "not applicable" when appropriate.

One final point about the bases for our effect ratings: to the extent that a given review examined the same data as a prior review, and did not give any convincing new interpretation, we tried to reflect that in our ratings.

A. VARIABLE: DEGREE OF ORIGINAL LEARNING/MASTERY LEVEL

In Table A-2 there is near unanimity in the conclusion that the degree or level of original learning is probably the most potent influence on LTR. For example, Gardlin and Sitterley (1972) conclude, for motor tasks, that the level of initial mastery is the principal predictor of skill retention for any given interval. The overall potency of this variable is highlighted by the fact that all but one strength-of-effect ratings are 4s and 5s; and even that one exception is a 3.

Schendel, Shields and Katz (1978) echo the Gardlin and Sitterley (1972) conclusion, for motor learning, about the dominant effect of OL; Prophet (1976) and Hurlock and Montague (1982) agree that it applies to all kinds of learning. The latter authors go one step further, contending that "...any variable that leads to high initial levels of learning, such as high ability or frequent practice, will facilitate skill retention" (p. 5).

Given the undeniable relationship between the degree of OL and retention, it follows that one way to cut down on K&S decay is to "strengthen" the degree of OL. Most of the studies performed to explore this relationship increase the degree of OL by providing extra practice or trials before retention is assessed. When these supplementary trials are given in a laboratory or other controlled setting, they typically are added *after* the trainee has achieved a pre-set criterion of mastery -- usually the first fully-error-free performance trial. We will refer to this criterion of acquisition as *minimal mastery* because the evidence

47

shows that some non-trivial proportion of learners who reach this minimal mastery level will make a mistake on the very next trial.

For example, Rigg and Gray (1981) used a mastery-criterion level of three successive correct trials for U.S. Army enlisted personnel learning a procedural task. Ten percent of the soldiers committed errors between their first correct trial and their third successively correct trial. Rigg and Gray considered these soldiers as not having really learned the task, and declared that they (Rigg & Gray) were able, by using initial training-performance data and a Markov chain model, to predict what percent of the trainees would *really* master the task, that is, would be able to achieve, immediately after their first errorless trial, two more successive correct trials. In the case noted above, where they found 10% of the trainees deficient in terms of their arbitrary mastery criterion, Rigg and Gray claimed that their model predicted a 14% "failure rate." Unfortunately, these authors do not provide the reader with enough information about exactly how the initial performance data were employed by the model to generate the percentage rates.

What the Rigg and Gray (1981) study *does* illustrate, rather dramatically, is the arbitrary nature of a mastery criterion. For the vast majority of studies which have generated the data on the effects of various acquisition conditions and levels on retention, the mastery criterion has usually been a minimal one, set for convenience and practicality, not for any pedagogically-grounded reason. *Overlearning*, since it is conceptualized in relation to *post*-mastery learning, is as equally arbitrary as the typical mastery criterion. The amount of overlearning is usually expressed in terms of the number of trials beyond mastery, or as some additional percent of learning, e.g., 200% means that one receives double the number of trials that he took to achieve minimal mastery.

Because of the different levels at which we can operationally define mastery and overlearning, it follows that a trial that is part of the acquisition phase for one definitional situation can be part of the retention phase for another. For example, suppose we teach two groups of equated trainees the same material by the same method, with only one difference: members of Group A are said to have attained mastery when they perform their first errorless trial. The other group, Group B, is not deemed to have mastered the material until they correctly carry out three consecutive trials. If we now give those individuals from Group A who have reached their particular criterion level of mastery one additional trial, following immediately after their learning trials, we produce overlearning. But we can just as easily count this overlearning trial for Group A *as if it was a test of retention*, e.g., the first trial in a relearning-test paradigm.

Now, for convenience, let's call the number of the trial in which mastery is obtained (by any stated criterion) trial $\underline{m}$. As we have just seen, trial $\underline{m} + 1$ for Group A can easily be the same sequential trial as trial $\underline{m} - 2$ for Group B. Yet, if we were to be drawing curves of acquisition and immediate retention based on these two groups, these *equivalent* trials would be assigned to *different* curves: Group A's data, up to trial $\underline{m}$, would be reflected in an *acquisition* curve, whereas its data from trial $\underline{m} + 1$ would be part of a *forgetting* curve. In contrast, all of the trials through trial $\underline{m}$ for Group B would be considered part of the acquisition cycle.

Now, let's suppose that we gave Group A its $\underline{m} + 1$ trial after an hour, a week or a month had elapsed. Does this delayed extra trial produce overlearning in the same way, with the same effect on retention, as it does when it is contiguous with the learning trials? We do not know the answer to this fundamental, apparently elementary question. Probably, we would guess, there is no simple answer because the time interval, the task type and complexity, and the real degree of original learning, *inter alia*, can all simultaneously influence the outcome.

We have stated above that the relevant literature heavily supports the prescription that forgetting can be slowed down by increasing the degree of original learning. We have seen that how one defines when original learning has occurred, and how one quantifies the degree or level of original learning is problematical. The arbitrary aspects, perhaps, need not be so arbitrary. It is possible to measure the degre of OL in ways other than trials taken, time spent or number of errors made until acquisition has been achieved. Jones (1985), for example, proposes a stabilization-error theory of retention based on recent data indicating that acquisition has not really been "completed" until the learning curve slope has begun to level off. He suggests, therefore, that the shape of the learning curve, as well as the trainee's approximation to some arbitrary criterion, would yield a more stable and accurate prediction of LTR. In this connection, see the discussion by Lane (in press) of conditions that affect curve shape, especially the part dealing with "insight" learning and "all or none" learning.

It is also desirable, for certain critical skills such as flying an aircraft or executing emergency procedures, to require a level of mastery approaching automaticity of performance, akin to running off a thoroughly overlearned program which requires little conscious effort (Shiffrin & Schneider, 1977; Schneider, Dumais & Shiffrin, 1984). Although not particularly practical, one could continue to sample the individual's spare cognitive capacity by imposing a secondary-task loading while he is learning. A desirable or required level of mastery might be reached at the point that neither task seems to impose a performance decrement on the other .

B. INCREASING THE DEGREE OF ORIGINAL LEARNING (FUNCTIONAL EQUIVALENTS OF OVERLEARNING)

In addition to these alternative ways of indexing how much learning (or progress towards asymptotic performance) has occurred, there are several other ways of "strenthening" learning and thus retarding decay, than the overlearning brought about directly by additional practice. In the usual experimental situation for studying overlearning, one receives supplementary practice trials or sessions on the same materials or skills.

In contrast, Battig (1972) showed that subjects acquire more decay-resistant K&S by having to *overcome* high intratask interference during learning. That this learning outcome can be viewed as *functionally equivalent* to overlearning has been supported by the improved retention (and, to a lesser extent, improved positive transfer) that has been found (Battig, 1972; Hiew, 1977). Battig's objective with this approach was *specifically* to promote *retention*, as opposed to learning. His early studies, reported in his 1972 article, dealt exclusively with sources of interference intrinsic to the learning task, materials and procedure. He speculated that the improved retention came about because the individual would have to call on "additional learning processes" (p. 155) to successfully compete with the intratask interference. The resulting reduction in forgetting occurs because the "...additional learning [presumably a product of the posited additional learning processes] makes the material more resistant also to whatever factors would cause it subsequently to be forgotten" (p. 155).

Battig (1979) subsequently expanded his earlier interpretation of intratask interference to cover more general "contextual interference," thus taking in factors extraneous, as well as intrinsic, to the knowledge or skill being learned. Contextual interference was said to derive from changes across trials in the experimental context.

50

Battig proposed that such interference influenced learners to use multiple and variable strategies to encode the material being learned. Practice under this apparent handicap yields more elaborate and distinctive processing, and thus promotes long-lasting retention. We have already noted, several times before, that elaborations during processing produce KRRSs which are richer and more "discriminable," and hence lead to easier retrieval. Positive transfer is fostered to the extent that the contextual interference induces processing strategies appropriate for learning other material.

Shea and Morgan (1979) applied Battig's conceptualization to the retention and transfer of a motor skill. They measured retention after a 10-minute or a 10-day interval, and under either the same or different contextual conditions as those of the learning phase. Subsequent transfer to a task of either the same or greater complexity than the originally learned tasks was also measured. Results supported the Battig view. Retention (in terms of total time to perform the tasks) was higher following high interference during learning than after low interference when retention was measured under changed contextual-interference conditions. Similarly, transfer was better for the high-interference groups, and most striking for the transfer task of greatest complexity.

This support, in the domain of motor skills, for Battig's unique approach to promoting LTR and transfer, should be especially interesting from a theoretical aspect. From a practical standpoint, the extra time presumably needed by the learner to overcome the introduced interference might not be at all cost effective. That question, however, remains an empirical one: we would need to contrast experimentally the Battig approach (one of essentially increasing the degree of OL) to overlearning and to other functional equivalents of overlearning (which we will take up shortly).

C. THE THEORETICAL ROLE OF REHEARSAL AND REPETITION

Returning to the theoretical implications of the Battig conceptualization, we see here an analog to overlearning. In the case of standard overlearning, however, the salutary effect on retention is generally attributed merely to the effects of additional repetitions, of a strengthening of connections due directly to the rehearsal or practice per se, with no mediating processing proposed to explain the effect. On the contrary, we believe that the quality of the processing during overlearning, as well as during OL, contributes importantly to the memorability of the K&S learned. We support the cognitive viewpoint: that the learner is always actively processing information when he is awake and interacting with his environment. It follows that the learner's attempts to organize and transform what he is trying to learn take place just as actively and productively during overlearning trials as during initial acquisition trials. Mandler (1968) represents this point of view strongly, asserting that the role of time or repetition is to enable the learner to reorganize larger subjective units. "Repetition, or rather time, permits the subject to lay down initial categories and to fit items into them or to reorganize the categories" (p. 116). Mandler then makes an interesting point about individual differences, a topic we will consider later. He argues that the time required to form a stable organization of a particular set of items will vary from person to person, "depending on pre-established organizations, i.e., past experience, as well as pre-established, possibly innate, organizational factors" (p. 116).

Mandler (1968) makes another point so unequivocally that it warrants a direct quotation because of its bluntness: "I reject the rehearsal notion, if for no other reason than that rehearsal does not produce recall; only organization does. Rehearsal is a descriptive term" (p. 117). This unconditional assertion would imply that the sheer acts of practice and rehearsal do not by themselves produce a retrievable trace.

D.   INCIDENTAL LEARNING AND PROCESSING DEMANDS

Mandler's position seems too rigid. Among other things, it would seem to deny the existence of *incidental* learning, to leave it unexplained, unless Mandler would contend that all material encountered, registered, learned and remembered is organized, consciously or unconsciously, even if there is no *intention* to learn. To us, incidental learning is an undeniable phenomenon, although it is difficult to explain in a cognitive framework. It is a form of learning which "*apparently* (italics added) takes place without a specific motive or a specific formal instruction and set to learn the activity or material in question" (McGeoch & Irion, 1952, p. 210).

Incidental learning poses theoretical problems because a great deal of what comes within our sensory range is *not* absorbed and remembered. Why is certain material acquired and retained although it does not seem to be any more important or conspicuous than the other sensory information available at the same time? Unfortunately many experiments reported under the topic of incidental learning are methodologically flawed, claim McGeoch and Irion (1952), because they fail to exclude from the learning situation all forms of motivation and reinforcement which might affect acquisition. However, there are experiments (e.g., Shellow, 1923; Biel & Force, 1943) which do not contain any experimental flaws and yet found apparently conclusive evidence in support of incidental learning. In fact, the Biel and Force study found that, when level of learning was controlled, the material learned under incidental conditions was retained as well as intentionally learned material.

Given that we accept incidental learning as an indisputable phenomenon, it would strongly suggest that learning can indeed occur without conscious processing of what is being acquired and stored. It would, consequently, follow that *some* learning is a function of mere exposure, plus a minimal degree of attention, to a stimulus. And it further follows that *repeated* exposures ought to strengthen that learning and thereby promote retention. We all have learned phone numbers or addresses of friends although we had no intention of committing them to memory. Most of us are easily able to recognize the voice of certain telephone callers after only one or two words -- but we never practiced or consciously processed the phonemic traces of their sound, intonation or inflection.

We propose the following cognitively-oriented explanation of incidental learning. There are different kinds and degrees of information processing, usually determined by the intent of the processor. Experiments supporting the existence of incidental learning all tried to ensure that the subjects *attend* to the incidental material while, at the same time, not acquire a "set" to learn it. We would argue that the act of attending to the material for some purpose necessarily entails *some* processing as the subject mentally manipulates the material. Although this processing is not strategically intended to promote retention, successful incidental learning occurs when the number, variety and depth of the encoding traces are "strong" enough to link up with one or more KRRSs (which, of course, are already planted in long-term memory). These KRRSs may contain traces relating habitual ways of thinking, of dealing with apparently extraneous information, of interpreting instructions, or of inferring meaning. Thus, the KRRSs invoked or "primed" by the incidental learning stimuli may themselves further influence one's set as to how to deal with the material.

53

For example, Postman and Sanders (1946) report that their experimental subjects may have had "covert sets" (not necessarily within their awareness) that operated to produce incidental learning. McGeoch and Irion (1952) state that these covert sets are of "undoubted importance in incidental learning experiments" (p. 214). These investigators cite an example of a case in which the subject is instructed to read, but not instructed to memorize the material. In spite of the lack of instructions, the subject learns and retains the incidental material because he has an "implicit set toward memorization" (p. 214). This implicit set is the product of well-established reading habits which tend to make the subject process the material being read *as if* he needs to understand and retain it. Indeed, as we shall discuss later, the act of merely trying to *understand* (without an intention to commit to memory) may well yield the kinds of qualitatively rich, elaborative-processing products that automatically promote retention by facilitating retrieval.

We have presented evidence that making the learner "work harder," to overcome contextual interference, improves LTR. We agree with the interpretation of Battig (1979) and Shea and Morgan (1979) that this improvement is most likely caused by enhanced processing which leads to more accessible retrieval structures. We have also just presented some evidence for, and some theoretically-grounded explanation of, how incidental learning can produce a stable memory trace. These two kinds of learning are examples of widely contrasting situations. In the case of having to overcome contextual interference, the learner is forced to attend to and "deeply process" the material to be learned. In the case of the incidental learning, acquisition seems to come about effortlessly. The conspicuous divergence of these two approaches to learning and memory serves to set the stage for, and highlight, the next topic: the role of effort in learning and remembering.

E.   THE CONCEPT OF COGNITIVE EFFORT

The cognitive effort expended in learning and remembering is a difficult concept to deal with unless it is (a) operationally defined, and (b) able to be related to similar concepts, such as the level of processing (LOP). In this section, we will not deal with all the ramifications of the LOP approach, first named and popularized by Craik and Lockhart (1972) as a framework for memory research. We will save our extended discussion of the LOP construct, and the work it has spawned, for a later section on instructional design and strategies. In that context, it will be considered as the primary variable which can be most profitably manipulated to enhance learning, retention and positive transfer.

F.   COGNITIVE EFFORT AND LEVELS OF PROCESSING

As Tyler, Hertel, McCallum and Ellis (1979) observe, the cognitive-effort concept needs to be looked at in the context of the LOP approach. We will therefore provide enough background about it now to help establish this context. The LOP approach emphasizes the nature of knowledge represented and the encoding operations of the learner. The notion is that people employ a series of mental analyzers, varying along a continuum from structural (nonsemantic) to semantic analysis, in processing any material they want to store in memory. Semantic analyses involve encoding attributes of the *meaning* of the to-be-learned material. Nonsemantic features, such as a word's spelling, do not involve an item's meaning.

The LOP concept maintains that, within this layered continuum, the greater the depth to which an item is processed, the greater is the probability that it will be later retrievable. If repetition ensures only that the item keeps being processed to the same depth, memory is not improved beyond the level associated with that depth.

A number of experiments (Mistler-Lachman, 1974; Craik & Tulving, 1975; Bower & Karlin, 1974) support the LOP concept, especially confirming that semantic coding results in higher recall and recognition than nonsemantic coding, no matter what the intentions of the learners are. However, the LOP viewpoint was attacked (Nelson, 1977; Baddeley, 1978) because it did not include any way of defining the different *levels* of processing independently of the memorial consequences, that is, of arranging different tasks in some consistent order along the depth continuum. Further, Nelson (1977) contended that it can be empirically shown that *repeated* processing of an item, to the *same* depth, does, in fact, yield improved memory as compared to non-repeated processing.

In an attempt to overcome these limitations of the LOP concept, Tyler et al. (1979) proposed *cognitive effort* as a conceptual equivalent. Explicitly, they defined it as the amount of the available processing capacity of the individual used in carrying out an information-processing task. How does one measure this quantity? The general approach is based on divided attention, in which the subject concurrently performs a primary task (e.g., motor tracking) and a secondary task (e.g., one involving measuring simple reaction time to auditory or visual stimuli). [See Kerr, 1973, for a review of secondary-task paradigms.] How well a subject performs on the secondary task is an indicator of how much effort he is expending on the primary processing task. The assumption is that the greater the proportion of one's limited-capacity, central-processing capability required for the primary task, the poorer will be the performance on the secondary task.

How do we tell which manipulations of tasks, stimulus attributes, or instructional strategies correspond to manipulations of effort? The answer by Tyler et al. (1979) lies in evaluating the effects, on the secondary task, of varying the processing demands of the primary task. For example, one group of subjects, in the primary anagram task, had to unscramble a series of letters which were scrambled only slightly (the low-effort condition); the other group represented the high-effort condition because the letters required extensive rearrangement. Measurements of secondary-task proficiency confirmed that significantly longer time was taken to respond successfully to secondary-task probe stimuli for subjects engaged in the high-effort task than for those performing the low-effort task.

Tyler et al. (1979) found, by using this divided-attention paradigm, that recall of items processed during high-effort conditions was significantly better than recall for low-effort conditions. In discussing the possible mechanism by which more effort seems to produce improved recall, the investigators posit two choices. Greater effort may produce a greater tendency to integrate the context (the task environment) and the task components to be recalled, thereby facilitating later retrieval. Alternatively, "it might be the case that an item in a higher-effort situation is stored in memory as a trace of greater strength" (p. 616).

G. EXPENDED-PROCESSING CAPACITY

A somewhat different approach to the cognitive effort notion is that of *expended-processing capacity* (EPC) (Johnston, Griffith & Wagstaff, 1972). EPC in some sense is conceived of as the "ease" of recall: the extent to which retrieval from memory demands or consumes processing capacity. We can, using this concept, regard the process of searching for a memory trace as varying in the degree to which it is accurate, fast, and requires processing capacity.

Johnston et al. (1972) used the concurrent-primary-and-secondary-task methodology [as in the Tyler et al. (1979) paradigm just described] to measure how much of a subject's processing capacity was used up by the primary task. However, unlike the Tyler et al. study, the primary task in the Johnston et al. approach was one of memory retrieval, not of acquisition. EPC was measured as reaction time to light signals which were presented simultaneously with specific retrieval demands. Thus, it was assumed that the more intense the memory search required for recall, the longer should be the subject's reaction time be to the subsidiary task's demands. Johnston et al. conclude, and cite eight studies to support their contention, that "...there is substantial evidence that the EPC measure is both feasible and useful" (p. 512).

In their experiments, these researchers obtained EPC data during *input* as well as during retrieval. Their results strongly suggested that *encoding* requires less EPC than information *retrieval*. The EPC measure also proved to be greater for incorrect recall than for correct recall, indicating the possibility that erroneous retrieval leads to more processing.

We have described the EPC approach because it holds out promise of an additional unbiased tool for studying processing effort. Since it can be measured at any point in the information-processing chain, it can serve as objective evidence of certain theory-based hypotheses about the strength or degree of encoding for different kinds of tasks which vary in complexity and type. Furthermore, ease of recall, as assessed by EPC, can be considered an additional measure (supplementing accuracy and latency data) of retention. Although EPC will not tell us *what* is retained, we can say that item x seems to be represented as a "stronger" trace than item y if less EPC is used up in retrieving trace x as compared to trace y. It follows that we could, by this *objective* measure, order sets of material learned to different arbitrary criteria, including "overlearning criteria," on a scale of EPC measures.

The concept of cognitive effort leads logically to the question we have already posed several times: What is the role that sheer repetition or rehearsal plays? By adding the effort concept to the rehearsal concept, all that is being implied is that "more effortful" rehearsal or practice promotes retention. Such a position does little theoretically. Rather, it leaves wide open the question of the various cognitive operations that are occurring during the time that the individual is processing information while exerting differential effort.

Empirically, as well as intuitively, the notion that learning with more effort leads to stronger memorial products cannot be dismissed. We have seen that overcoming contextual interference leads to improved LTR. We have also observed that everyday life provides us with numerous examples of successful incidental learning and LTR of the products of that learning. There clearly appears to be an effect of sheer, consistent exposure *qua* exposure to material, where there is no overt intention to learn, that sometimes leads to acquisition and relatively stable retention. In addition, there is no denying that, for many adults and children, especially in an academic setting, a non-trivial proportion of what they learn is acquired through drill and practice, a technique that seems to depend on the extent of repetition which, in turn, relates to amount of effort and time spent.

H. TIME AND THE DEGREE OF PROCESSING

Logically, it would appear that, no matter whether frequent repetition results in a brute-force strengthening of an associative relationship, or an opportunity for more elaborative, deeper processing, a plausible candidate for an independent correlate of processing depth is *time*. Nevertheless, time has not been found to predict memorial stability (Craik & Tulving, 1975, Kunen, Green, & Waterman, 1979), in that increases in processing time have not consistently been correlated with improved retention. In fact, Craik & Tulving (1975) claim that the difficulty or level of the encoding task is more predictive of retention than is the amount of time spent in processing an item. Using an incidental-learning task, they encountered subjects who made semantic judgments (a presumably deep level of processing) more rapidly than subjects who judged whether letters were upper or lower case (a presumably shallow-processing level). Yet the semantic-processing, faster subjects had higher recall scores.

If time *per se* is to serve as an independent index of the degree or depth of processing, it is important to be precise about what is actually being timed. Before employing time to compare subjects' performance between and within tasks, one should realize that we have no common underlying metric or scale with which to equate units of processing time across different tasks. If we consider as equivalent a minute of semantic processing, for example, with a minute of non-semantic processing, we are wrongly assuming that the underlying encoding processes are qualitatively similar.

58

I.   INDUCING INCREASED PROCESSING AND IMPROVED RETENTION BY TASK MANIPULATION

So far we have seen that the level or degree of original learning can be measured, or at least conceptualized, in terms of (a) the amount of practice or number of trials spent in reaching a pre-defined criterion of accuracy or speed; (b) the apparent additional processing that a learner must engage in so that he can successfully overcome intratask or contextual interference; and (c) the cognitive effort or mental capacity involved in encoding material for later retrieval. There is no conclusive basis for arguing that more enduring retention can be achieved *only* by intensive and elaborative processing. However, evidence has been presented to support the view that the intensity and quality of processing are the *primary* factors required for ensuring LTR.

Certainly the ways just mentioned for increasing the amount or level of OL can all be interpreted as approaches to inducing, or providing additional opportunity for, richer, deeper, more elaborative processing. The contextual-interference paradigm appears to force the learner to make finer discriminations in order to repel competing and potentially intrusive associations. Kunen, Green & Waterman (1979) required their learners to identify degraded stimuli (outline drawings which varied in how complete their contours were). Their hypothesis, which was supported by their results, was straightforward: as the contour impoverishment increased, more extensive or elaborative processing would be needed to reconstitute the whole picture for successful identification. The consequence of this enhanced processing would be improved retention. To Kunen et al., the kind of higher-quality encoding that their incomplete stimuli induced represented a wider *spread* of processing. This notion, referred to as the "spread of encoding," was formulated by Craik and Tulving (1975) in response to the criticisms made of Craik and Lockhart's (1972) *depth* of processing concept.

The spread of encoding yields improved memory resulting from an elaboration of processing operations conducted *within* one distinct level or domain. In the Kunen et al. (1979) experiments, the spread of encoding was operationally defined as reaction time to identify the drawings accurately. The results were clear and statistically significant: subjects whose reaction times for identifying the incomplete drawings were slowest (indicating they had had to engage in more elaborative processing) were best able to

59

recognize the fragmented drawings when they were presented along with similar, but not previously shown pictures.

In addition to the support that the Kunen et al. results provide to the importance of elaborative processing (whether one chooses to call it speed or depth) for retention, their study illustrates the unusual potency of the processing notion in the following respect. Traditional views hold that one's memory for stimuli improves as the stimuli increase in clarity and completeness. Yet, the data of Kunen and his associates reveal that, in certain circumstances, the quality and extent of cognitive analyses used by subjects to make sense out of stimuli can overpower the attributes of clarity and completeness.

An interesting point about the Kunen et al. study is worth noting: it illustrates dramatically that strong retention-improving processing can be effectively induced by the perceived qualities and demands of the task -- it does not need to be induced by instructional strategies. (Later, when we discuss retention as a function of the type and characteristics of the learning task, this point will be better appreciated.)

J.   INDUCING INCREASED PROCESSING AND IMPROVED RETENTION BY CRITERION MANIPULATION

The Kunen et al. (1979) study just discussed manipulated the learner's task, "forcing" him, in effect, to "perceptually analyze" and reconstruct the stimuli in order to identify them. Since those individuals who had to successfully analyze the most degraded pictures showed the best retention, the authors concluded that the extra processing led to more elaborated KRRSs which, in turn, produced better retention.

Although we agree with the Kunen et al. interpretation, it is still possible that the extra processing time and effort invested in disambiguating the incomplete stimuli led to merely stronger, and hence more durable traces. We propose, therefore, that it might be possible to induce retention-facilitating processing by manipulating the difficulty level of the mastery criterion. For example, if the real-life requirements demanded that a soldier should be able to disassemble and reassemble a submachine gun in m minutes with no errors, the mastery criterion could be set at $m - .20m$, requiring, in other words, that he perform the same task to the same degree of accuracy in 20% less time.

Another example: If we want soldiers learning to shoot a rifle to be able to place 7 out of 10 shots within a target circle of d diameter, from y yards, let us change the mastery criterion, purely for learning and retention purposes, to one requiring hitting the correct zone 9 out of 10 tries, from $y + 10$ yards.

We cannot find any studies in the literature bearing on this particular way of making the learner "work harder" so that he can reach a higher level of mastery. We believe that experiments could profitably be conducted that would compare the effects of the kinds of mastery-level changes we suggest with those obtained by the standard overlearning paradigm of providing additional trials or practice beyond minimal mastery. Our first hypothesis would be that those learners achieving the more rigorous criterion would retain more of the essential K&S demanded by the job, i.e., required for merely achieving the lesser criterion of mastery, than would trainees learning only to minimal mastery. Our second hypothesis would say that the degree of "overmastery" accomplished by meeting the more difficult or more arduous criterion could be set at a level which would make it functionally equivalent, in terms of retarding decay, to a certain level of traditionally defined overlearning.

The *practical* questions here, of course, assuming that our notion is valid, are how much extra time and related resources would be needed to train the learner to the more difficult criterion, and would it be cost effective. Two *theoretically* interesting questions are intriguing: (a) If we get a positive memory-enhancement effect from our suggested manipulation, is it due to more processing of the to-be-learned material, or is it a result of straightforwardly strengthened traces which are thus less vulnerable to decay and/or interference; and (b) Will the forgetting curve of the "overmastery" group be different than the comparable curve for the more traditional overlearning group?

Why have we brought up this "overmastery" notion and suggested a line of research at this point in this report? One answer is that we perceive of overmastery as a functional equivalent of overlearning, and it thus belongs in this section (even though it is somewhat speculative). The direction of research we proposed in connection with it would shed much-needed light on the theoretical issue of "quality vs. strength" of processing as determinants of durable retention. We posed that problem earlier when we addressed the question of the role of repetition or rehearsal.

K. DEGREE OF ORIGINAL LEARNING AND FIDELITY OF SIMULATION

When simulation is used for training, the question of the most effective degree of fidelity of simulation always arises. There is a separate body of literature bearing on that question, and it is outside the scope of this paper to deal with that material at any length. However, in keeping with our argument that the quality and intensity of one's encoding is probably the primary determinant of the memorability of the encoded material, we believe fidelity of simulation can be looked at in terms of the number and richness of the KRRSs formed. Where simulation is used to convey procedural relationships and sequences, or to teach conceptual understandings, it functions pedagogically like any other medium for instruction. To the extent that it causes the trainee to process effectively what is being learned, the trainee will form *qualitatively superior* KRRSs. Admittedly, that is a tautological explanation, because we have no independent way of operationally defining "qualitatively superior." For the moment, however, we are being speculative, based on our belief that those KRRSs that are most accessible for retrieval are those formed by some optimal mix of intensive and extensive processing -- referring both to the *depth* and *spread* of encoding elaborations. (We will further discuss the issue of how to best define, or at least infer, *qualitatively* superior encoding, under the topic of instructional design strategies.)

To provide some evidence for our proposition that the fidelity-of-simulation issue can be usefully illuminated by considering the underlying processing operations and knowledge-representation, we selected a study by Grimsley (1969) to present in chart form (see Table B-1).

It represents a solid experimental attempt to examine the effects of varying the degree of fidelity of simulation on LTR. The experiment used soldiers learning a complex procedural military task involving tactical equipment. Yet, as Table B-1 reveals, there were no significant acquisition or retention differences found, after 4 and 6 weeks, among three groups of trainees who had received training under different levels of simulation. It is certainly conceivable that these varying degrees of simulation did not lead to any functionally different KRRSs. Consequently, retrieval success should not be differentially influenced.

Simulation of training environments and tasks which involve motor learning is more difficult to address from the standpoint of processing and representation. Early in this report, we commented on how little is known about how human motor memory is compiled and represented in trace-network form. In the motor domain, it is intuitively eaiser to accept the belief that sheer repetition, leading to a straightforward strengthening of connections, is a potent, if not the most crucial determinant of enduring skill retention. Personal experience tells us that the more we practice, the faster we learn and the better we retain. It is difficult to believe that one forms many cognitive elaborations in learning, for example, to ride a bicycle. It appears that we will need to know quite a bit more about the nature of motor memory before we can apply the qualitative-processing approach to prescriptions for its improvement.

L.   RECENT STUDIES ON "STANDARD" OVERLEARNING

The issue of why and how overlearning increases memory durability is obviously related to the question of decay rates as a function of different degrees of original acquisition.

If the degree of OL is the sole or primary determinant of LTR, then inducing overlearning (whether by the standard technique of additional trials, or by use of the functional equivalents we have discussed) should be our most valuable instructional treatment for ensuring LTR. From a practical standpoint, overlearning is indeed a reliable way of strengthening retention. However, the literature shows that providing overlearning trials runs into a point of diminishing returns (McGeoch & Irion, 1952). For example, Kroeger (1929) had his subjects overlearn by 150% and 200%, and tested them on the lists of monosyllabic nouns after intervals of 1, 2, 4, 7, 14 and 28 days. Both degrees of overlearning led to an increase in recall and savings scores after each interval, but the increase was smaller from 150% to 200% than from 100% (minimal mastery) to 150%.

Underwood and Keppel (1963), basing their conclusions mostly on verbal, list learning, maintained that the greater the degree of learning, the slower should be the rate of forgetting. Their explanation for this was that repeated trials not only fortify the strength of the associations, but also increase the extinction of potentially interfering responses.

All these assertions about the relationship between the degree of OL and the rate of decay seem to assume that the learned material is forgotten as a unit. We would maintain, on the contrary, that *complex* tasks (which we would define as those comprised of different types of components with different memorability attributes) decay differentially. We would further argue that some component skills may have been differentially learned, and thus may decay at different rates. For example, component skills which were trained in a variety of contexts (as we noted earlier when we discussed Battig's (1979) notion of contextual interference) are more likely to endure. Similarly, skill and knowledge components which are processed more elaborately or effortfully should be less vulnerable to decay.

What does the recent literature tell us about *differential* forgetting rates? Christiaansen (1980) tested recognition of prose passages over intervals of 1 week, 1 month and 2 months, and found no evidence of different forgetting rates. In summarizing the relevant literature, however, he noted that three other studies using free recall of prose passages revealed that thematically important ideas are forgotten at a slower rate than less relevant ideas. Christaansen's explanation of why he chose to use recognition as his retention-measuring method is interesting, because it illustrates a property of memory that is, we believe, one of its major intrinsic characteristics: memory is both *reconstructive* (e.g., see Bartlett, 1932; Sachs, 1967; Bransford & Johnson, 1972; Loftus & Palmer, 1979) and *reproductive* (e.g., see Cofer, Chmielewski & Brockway, 1976; Rubin, 1977), depending on the perceived situational demands. *Recall* of a text, states Christaansen, allows differential retrieval and reconstructive processes or strategies to operate at the time of output, i.e., at the time of the retention test. The problem is that "...there is no control over changes in the output processing strategies of subjects as the retention interval increases" (p. 612).

Recently, Slamecka and McElree (1983) had their subjects learn verbal material to different levels of acquisition, and tested them at periods ranging from immediately following acquisition to 5 days afterwards. The experimenters concluded that forgetting was independent of the acquisition level because the difference in retention scores on the items learned to different levels was as large after long delays as after short delays.

When G. Loftus (1985) analyzed the Slamecka & McElree data, he arrived at the *opposite* conclusion because of a different perspective. Loftus measured how much time it takes for retention to fall from a stated level to some lower level. Whenever such decay times differed, he considered the decay rates as being different. Based on this viewpoint, he found that it took less time for a drop from one level of retention to a lower retention level when the amount of OL was lower. His conclusion, therefore, was that forgetting is slower for more overlearned material and skills. We believe that the Loftus reinterpretation is legitimate, and that it reemphasizes the point we have stressed repeatedly -- that K&S, in whole *or* as component parts, can be learned to various criterion levels, and that these different levels will affect how much and how long the K&S are sustained.

M. EFFECT OF PRIOR KNOWLEDGE ON THE ORIGINAL LEARNING-RETENTION RELATIONSHIP

Mastery learning typically refers to learning that sets specific mastery criteria for every module in an individualized or self-paced instructional program. It assumes that the speed and mode of learning are not important. Instead, the emphasis is on the goal that each student master certain information at his own rate. It is assumed that material that is well learned will be equally well remembered, independent of learning conditions. However, E. Gagne et al. (1985) had middle-school students learn paragraphs on topics of high or moderate familiarity (meaningfulness, prior knowledge). The students were tested for recall either several minutes or 4 weeks after learning. The results showed that the element of familiarity influenced both speed of OL and the amount recalled. Gagne et al. suggest that two students (with different amounts of prior knowledge on a topic) who reach the same level of mastery on the topic in a mastery learning program will not retain equal amounts of the material over time. Gagne and her associates further suggest that prior knowledge not only influences the quantity of learning per unit time, but also the quality. And these qualitative differences, they assert, lead to differential retrievability of information. They note also that their obtained pattern of results is consistent with the notion [see Ausubel (1969); Anderson & Reder (1979)] that learners confronting more familiar and meaningful material find it easier to form more structured and elaborate traces because the existing related knowledge provides an "ideational scaffolding" for new information. And this scaffolding leads to more stable, more permanent, and more distinctive traces.

65

N. OVERLEARNING: THE EFFECT OF VARYING ITS POINT OF INTRODUCTION

Before we leave the general topic of the relationship between the degree of OL and the course of retention, one more piece of experimentally-derived data is worth discussing. Schendel & Hagman (1982) [Table B-2] took the unusual step of introducing "extra" learning trials to one group of soldiers 4 weeks after minimal mastery of a procedural task. Except for the timing, the authors considered that these extra trials provided 100% overlearning. This particular "midway" overlearning group was then tested 4 weeks later. The other experimental group received the same degree of overlearning, but at a different point: immediately following the final acquisition trial. It was tested for retention at the same time that the midway overlearning group was tested, that is, 8 weeks after its contiguous learning and overlearning trials. Both overlearning groups, in comparison to a control group, showed significantly better retention. The traditional overlearning group retained the procedural components "marginally better" than the midway overlearning subjects.

Although the unusual design of the Schendel and Hagman experiment makes it difficult to interpret theoretically, the practical implication is quite clear. The degree of learning is far more important for LTR than is the time at which the additional trials are given. The authors assert that "Overtraining may be a potent avenue for reducing costs and increasing effectiveness, at least when sustaining procedural skills over a fixed retention interval" (p. 610).

The procedure used in the Schendel and Hagman study highlights the arbitrary nature of the boundary between acquisition and retention. The overlearning trials received by what we have termed the "midway group" (which could as well be referred to as the delayed-overlearning group) also can be regarded as a refresher-training session. The very interesting question then arises, which we have never seen explicitly voiced or confronted in the literature: Can not all "practice" or "refresher-training" trials, if they occur after acquisition, be regarded as the *equivalent* of overlearning trials? This question is obviously relevant to the problem of at what intervals should we provide refresher training or practice trials in order to keep a K or S from falling to an unacceptable decay level.

Bahrick (1979) conducted a study which was even more paradigmatically unorthodox than the Schendel and Hagman (1982) experiment. Superficially, it appears

66

that the Bahrick design sought to test the effects of spaced presentations of learning trials. Three groups of subjects, learning to recognize Chinese characters, had to select the correct answer from 5-multiple-choice candidates. Learning trials consisted of alternating presentations and test trials. On each learning trial (the "presentation trial"), items answered correctly on the prior test trial were dropped out. The subject therefore continued to be presented only with items that he had failed to recognize. *In each session*, all the subjects learned to a mastery criterion of one errorless trial.

Group 1 received seven training sessions at 30-day intervals. Group 2 was trained with a one-day interval separating its first 6 sessions; its last session occurred 30 days after its 6th session. Group 3 received its first 6 sessions with no intersession interval; its 7th and final session was presented as was that of Group 2, namely 30 days following the 6th session. Bahrick's unusual experimental design can be considered as stressing the impact of overlearning on retention. Groups 1 and 2, since they had learned to mastery at each successive session, were effectively taking a retention test, in each session, by relearning the task each time around. In apparent contrast, Group 3 was administered a continuous series of training trials, back to back, for six relearning sessions. (Conceivably, each session after the initial one could be completed in one trial.) Paradigmatically, *all* trials beyond initial mastery for Group 3 can be viewed as overlearning trials.

Bahrick chose to interpret his findings based solely on the difference, for each group, between the 6th session's scores and the retention score measure obtained 30 days later. He found that his subjects (a) maintained high retention across the long intersession periods; and (b) performed best in the final test session when the earlier intersession intervals were the longest--and therefore corresponded to the period between the last relearning session and the final test session. These results lead Bahrick to draw some conclusions which are extremely relevant to the problems of skill decay for the military community. If you want learners to retain information well, that is, suffer negligible decay over a particular time interval (say 30 days), then you should space out their "successive reacquisition sessions" (refresher training) with intervals of about the same length. Put another way, to maintain any given achieved K or S level over nonuse periods, you should provide a series of refresher training sessions at intervals as long as the desired maintenance period.

Bahrick's finding which is of most direct relevance to the overlearning/degree of OL issue was that performance in the final test session depended more on the *earlier* intersession intervals than on the level of retention performance achieved in the last relearning session. Here we have evidence that learners who demonstrate the same level of skill proficiency just after training can differ markedly on LTR, depending on their prior training history. This finding provides more reason to reject what we consider the simplistic view that one's level of OL, *taken by itself*, is an adequate predictor of LTR.

O. THE VARIABLE OF TASK CHARACTERISTICS (TYPE AND COMPLEXITY OF ORGANIZATION)

Most literature about this variable has tried to deal meaningfully with the wide variety of tasks by classifying them according to task type. Typically these categorizations are fairly gross, and include discrete motor/psychomotor tasks, continuous-control motor tasks, verbal tasks (ranging from lists of nonsense syllables to meaningful prose passages), and procedural tasks.

"The most important tasks in the Navy tend to be procedural in nature..." (Hurlock and Montague, 1982, p. VII). These types of tasks are probably equally prevalent and important across all services. There are other non-procedural tasks, such as landing on an aircraft carrier, troubleshooting complex equipment, and tactical decision making in a command-and-control context which are both mission-critical and difficult to master and retain.

Table A-3 reveals that all of the reviewers recognized two salient points relating to the memorability of tasks: (a) No matter what the task type, the *organizational complexity* of a task is the key task-specific determinant of LTR; and (b) there are few tasks in real life that are clearly of one "pure" type, and those studied in the experimental laboratory and the military classroom do not represent any greater degree of purity.

In spite of this purity issue, tasks which require predominantly continuous motor control are significantly better retained then discrete or procedural tasks (Naylor and Briggs, 1961; Prophet, 1976; Schendel, Shields and Katz, 1978). However, this conclusion is easily explainable in terms of task organization. As Table A-3 indicates, Naylor and Briggs (1961) recognized that the retention advantage for continuous motor tasks was probably caused by "task integration," i.e., the degree of internal organization or cohesiveness. Prophet (1976) agreed with the interpretation, and used the same reasoning to explain why procedural tasks generally show a rapid and steep decline in retention. The responsible factor in such tasks, Prophet stated, is their lack of internal organization. He believed that the poor retention found for instrument flying skills was probably due to their procedural task loading.

The organizational complexity or degree of cohesiveness of a task is undoubtedly, as Table A-3 confirms, a highly potent influence on LTR. Annett (1979) points out, however, that there is no satisfactory way of operationally defining this construct. In fact, contends Annett, variations in task organization may be viewed as equivalent to manipulations of task *difficulty*. As such, one may have to more intensively process the components of an organizationally complex task in order to learn it successfully. Such enhanced processing, as we emphasized earlier, can lead to an increase in the degree or level of OL that, in turn, promotes LTR. In other words, individuals who master poorly organized tasks are achieving a kind of functional equivalent of overlearning. As pointed out earlier in reference to work by Kunen, Green and Waterman (1979), memory performance increased for individuals who had to encode degraded, ambiguous pictures in order to reinstate their identity.

One might be tempted to claim, based on the kind of evidence just cited, that *any* tasks which are unusually difficult to learn will, *once learned*, be more resistant to forgetting than tasks more easily acquired to the same mastery criterion. This possibility is theoretically and intuitively appealing. It seems to follow a conservation law that the more you invest (in the form of cognitive effort), the greater is your return in the form of increased retention. However, we need definitive empirical evidence to confirm this assertion, and to clearly identify, for example, the relative contributions of the strength vs. the quality of any enhanced processing attributable to the extra difficulty.

Just as increased organization or cohesiveness serves to make a task more memorable, so too does the organizing effect of understanding. Apparently unrelated or ambiguously-related events in a story are analogous to steps, within a procedural task, that do not logically follow or cue each other. Yet, when the reader of such a fragmented passage is given relevant organizing information prior to reading the material, such information provides a coherent framework within which to better interpret the true meaning of the prose (Owens, Bower and Black, 1979). When the framework-providing orientation is also consistent with the learner's general knowledge of the world, recall is significantly improved (Morris, Stein and Bransford, 1979).

The evidence from the prose-learning literature supports drawing an analogy between the steps in a procedure and the sentences or episodes in a story. Horton and Mills (1984), in reviewing the very recent literature on human learning and memory, state that the evidence indicates that gist is remembered better than the surface details of sentences and stories, even though details are also remembered. Recall of both sentences and stories is enhanced when they are well integrated or more coherent. The authors conclude that "memory for sentences and stories, like memory for individual items, emphasizes the importance of organizational or relational processing of meaning" (p. 386).

Although many military tasks may be procedural in nature, they nevertheless represent a wide spectrum of types, difficulty, and memorability. To illustrate the contrast in memorability of two quite different kinds of military tasks, we have summarized experiments by Wertheim (1985) [Table B-3] and by Wetzel, Konoske and Montague (1983)[Table B-4]. Wertheim's trainees were either active-duty members of the Dutch Armed Services, or ex-conscripts who had been out of the Service for one year. Both groups had successfully completed the same army training and had the same amount of experience up to the point that the conscripts left the service. The task they had mastered was one that Wertheim claims focused on cognitive factors, i.e., on rules which, once acquired, are very well retained. The actual task required learning a sequence of procedural steps involved in shooting down enemy aircraft in a simulated, radar-aided, anti-aircraft weapon system. Each of the steps was quite simple to execute. In spite of a nonuse interval of one year, the ex-conscripts manifested no skill decay in accuracy or time to perform. Wertheim's explanation for this unusually durable retention is that if a task is largely characterized by an overall cohesive cognitive framework, forgetting will be negligible.

In contrast, the Wetzel et al. task proved to be difficult to retain. Sailors who had taken the Navy's 4-week course in sonar-signal processing (analyzing/classifying visual displays of acoustically-sensed information) were tested after a 25-day nonuse interval. The test results revealed significant decay for all of the three quite different sets of task characteristics: major components demanding knowledge or fact learning, computational-

70

skill acquisition, and mastery of procedures for classifying targets which vary greatly in their clarity and identifiability. This kind of task is probably an excellent example of a single task which taps different abilities, requires different kinds of learning (e.g., rote learning, procedural learning, and pattern recognition) and is not internally coherent. Merely appreciating the unusually complex and difficult nature of this task should have warned the training managers that the "built in" 25-day nonuse interval (before the trainees were scheduled to take a follow-on course) almost certainly augured marked degradation.

Another Army-sponsored study (Shields, Goldberg and Dressel, 1979) warrants discussion at this point because it provides valuable empirical data which relate certain organizational-coherence attributes of a variety of common U.S. soldier tasks (mainly procedural) to the decay rates of the attributes. (See Table B-5) The investigators concluded that the best predictor of the forgetting rate for an entire task was the number of steps required to perform the task. Furthermore, there were consistent findings, across 20 different tasks, revealing that what the soldiers tended to forget most were steps not cued by the prior steps or by the nature of the equipment itself.

Drawing upon the conclusions from the Shields, Goldberg and Dressel (1979) study, and from other research literature, Rigg (1983) [see Table B-6], at the request of the U.S. Army Training Board, derived an "index of task retention" to quantify the memorability of certain tasks (largely procedural) that were representative of a variety of U.S. Army military occupational specialties (MOSs). This index was created from research data which identified the seven task variables most often associated with skill decay. Each selected task was rated in terms of the extent to which it included one of the 7 decay-prone attributes. The resulting "task-categorization score" served as the basis for a relatively crude prediction of task retention. However, Rigg's approach did not yield any significant correlations, based on several weeks of nonuse, between the task-categorization scores and absolute retention scores. The Rigg technique did not include any weighting in terms of the *degree* to which each of the seven task variables characterized the task. This lack of weighting is probably the main reason for its failure to predict retention, although the technique could have possibly benefited by including other task attributes indexing memorability.

Based on recent work (Rose, Czarnolewski, Gragg, Austin, Ford, Doyle, & Hagman, 1984), a systematic and reportedly successful technique, derived from task characteristics related to internal organization, complexity and cohesiveness, has been formulated and demonstrated. How to use it is clearly and simply documented in a user's manual (Rose, Radtke, Shettel, and Hagman, 1985).

Each task is rated by cognizant personnel, preferably from the school offering the task training. The rater merely responds to one question on each of ten task attributes by providing a numerical scale score. When these scores are summed, the total constitutes the "retention rating score" for the task. A higher total predicts greater LTR.

The task properties tapped by the Rose et al. (1984) technique [which they call a "User's Decision Aid" (UDA)] either (a) resemble closely the organizational-complexity kind of characteristics we have been discussing, or (b) relate to factors which can make a task difficult to learn and remember, e.g., time pressure to complete it. For example, three items relate to attributes that are almost unique to a procedural task. These ask about the number of steps into which the task has been divided, their sequencing, and the extent of "built-in feedback so that you can tell if you are doing each step correctly" (Rose et al., 1985, p. 23). Other questions concern "mental processing requirements;" the requirement for *rote* memorization (both the amount and the difficulty of the rote material); the extent to which "job or memory aids" are used to perform the task; and the quality of any job aids used.

Several important points need to be made about the UDA prediction instrument.

1. It is useful primarily for procedural types of tasks.

2. The retention rating score (total score) for the task is easily converted to a "unit proficiency estimate" by merely referring to a simple look-up table [reproduced as Table 1, from Rose et al. (1985)]. This estimate predicts the "proportion of soldiers in a unit able to perform a task correctly after up to one year of no practice since a task was last performed correctly" (Rose et al., 1985, p. 37). For example, one would find that, for a total score of 150, 70% of soldiers could still be expected to perform the task correctly after 2 months of no practice. After 6 months of no practice on the same task, one would predict that only 34% of soldiers could perform it successfully.

3. The table could also be used to estimate how frequently refresher training should be provided to maintain proficiency at a given level, say 60%, for a

TABLE 1. TABLE FOR PREDICTING RETENTION DECAY BASED ON RATINGS OF SELECTED TASK CHARACTERISTICS

PERFORMANCE PREDICTION TABLE - MONTHS**

Total Score from Answer Sheet	Months Since Last Performance*											
	1	2	3	4	5	6	7	8	9	10	11	12
180+	100	100	100	100	100	100	100	100	100	100	100	100
175	97	95	92	90	87	85	83 .	81	79	77	75	73
170	94	90	85	81	76	72	69	65	62	59	56	53
165	92	85	78	72	66	61	56	52	48	44	40	37
160	89	80	71	64	57	51	45	40	36	32	29	26
155	86	75	64	56	48	42	36	31	27	23	20	17
150	83	70	58	49	40	34	28	24	20	16	14	11
145	80	65	52	42	34	27	22	17	14	11	9	7
140	77	60	46	36	27	21	16	12	10	7	6	4
135	74	55	40	30	22	16	12	9	6	5	3	2
130	70	50	35	25	17	12	8	6	4	3	2	1
125	67	45	30	20	13	9	6	4	2	1	1	0
120	63	40	25	16	10	6	4	2	1	1	0	0
115	59	35	20	12	7	4	2	1	0	0	0	0
110	54	29	16	8	4	2	1	0	0	0	0	0
105	50	25	12	6	3	1	0	0	0	0	0	0
100	44	20	8	4	1	0	0	0	0	0	0	0
95	38	15	2	0	0	0	0	0	0	0	0	0
90	31	10	3	1	0	0	0	0	0	0	0	0
85	22	5	1	0	0	0	0	0	0	0	0	0
80 or less	3	0	0	0	0	0	0	0	0	0	0	0

*Performance at "GO" level of Proficiency
**Taken from Rose, Radtke, Shettel, & Hagman, 1985, p. 40.

(Cell entries are the predicted proportions (percents) of soldiers in a unit able to perform the task correctly after the period of nonuse shown by the selected column.)

73

task for which the retention rating (total) score is 140. Looking along the row for the 140 value, we find the 60% figure in the column representing 2 months of no practice. The training manager is thus put on notice that this task needs to be refreshed every 2 months if he wants to ensure that at least 60% of a unit will be able to carry out the task successfully.

4.   The UDA has been validated against actual retention data collected from soldiers performing many different tasks that derive from several MOSs (Rose et al., 1984). Correlations in the neighborhood of r = .90 were obtained between actual retention performance and retention levels (accuracy and time) estimated by the UDA. Interrater reliability for assigning weightings to each task characteristic was relatively high, with an r value of .90+.

5.   In addition to existing in a paper-and-pencil version, by month (for up to 12 months) and by week (for up to 26 weeks) the UDA exists as a computerized version that can be implemented on an Apple microcomputer.

All in all, the UDA is a very promising algorithmic tool for predicting what proportion of a unit will remain proficient. However, the UDA does not tell us anything about any given individual's retention curve. Rose et al. (1984) examined this latter type of prediction, using actual soldier performance at acquisition as a predictor variable. More specifically, the performance-at-acquisition data were the number of inaccurate or omitted steps for the first trials in learning 22 Army procedural tasks. These tasks were tested at retention intervals of 2, 4 and 6 months.

Both the UDA task difficulty score and the first-trial-acquisiton data correlated significantly with performance at all retention periods. The UDA rating yielded generally superior prediction when averaged over all intervals. In addition, the UDA accounts for most of the variance that would have been predicted by the first-trial data alone. In short, "very little information is added by the inclusion of both variables" (Rose et al., 1984, p. 79). The critical issue here is that, in order to benefit from the relatively little remaining variance predicted by first-trial acquisition data, military training managers would have to gather the needed information through costly and time-consuming field trials--an impractical course of action, we believe.

P. VARIABLE: INSTRUCTIONAL STRATEGIES/CONDITIONS OF LEARNING

Considered broadly, as the major reviews surveyed in Table A-4 indicate, almost any condition of, or treatment imposed during, acquisition can have an effect on LTR. For present purposes, we will adopt this wide-sweeping view. It therefore follows that instructional-design ingredients such as sequencing, delivery systems, media, pacing, and mastery criteria, are all embraced by this variable. So too are major pedagogical approaches to instruction, including programmed instruction, computer-assisted instruction (CAI), computer-managed instruction (CMI), the extent and kind of simulation, and "top-down" (whole-task) training vs. "bottom-up" (part-task) approaches. Also included is the full range of instructional strategies, which may involve ways, for example, that the teacher (a) supplements the to-be-learned material; (b) adds explanations, examples and organization to foster both acquisition and retention; (c) suggests mnemonic aids to remembering; and (d) guides and interacts with the trainee adaptively (this includes the nature and amount of feedback provided).

Inspection of Table A-4 reveals that most of the instructional variables that are covered have been investigated primarily as learning, rather than memory variables (e.g., Schendel, Shields and Katz, 1978; Annett, 1979). Prophet (1976) does not even identify an instructional-treatment variable in his review. In his case, as with others, there is a definitional problem. He does not classify the degree of original learning, which is a function of the mastery criterion, as an instructional factor. [Table A-2 shows that the degree of OL (which may constitute overlearning) is probably the single best predictor of skill retention for any given time interval.] The decision by an instructional designer or teacher to set a particular criterion level of mastery should logically be a pedagogical one. However, because we have already treated the issue of overlearning and its analogs in quite some detail, it will not be further considered in this section.

Few clear patterns emerge from the reviews summarized in Table A-4 because the studies that were examined, for the most part, emphasized motor learning but neglected prose learning and complex-concept learning, where the effects of prior knowledge, expectations, meaningfulness/understanding, and semantic and structural complexity have been a major focus of investigation. The reader will recall that task complexity is a primary predictor for memory of procedural tasks. In fact, we believe that certain kinds of prose

75

learning can be functionally likened to procedural task learning. It can then be argued that *instructional interventions which have been shown to benefit the retention of information from prose passages should also facilitate the retention of procedural tasks.*

Procedural tasks are, by definition, a particular sequence of operations performed in the same fashion each time that the task is accomplished. Such tasks vary in several ways, e.g., (a) how many steps they require; (b) the extent to which executing one operation cues others; (c) the flexibility to deviate from a fixed sequence; (d) the amount of planning needed to perform the task; and (e) the number of decision points.

Although we can now predict the decay curve for many typical procedural tasks by using the UDA algorithm, this is an after-the-fact "fix." It is obviously much more desirable to protect procedural-task retention against decay by teaching a "fortified" set of less-likely-to-be-forgotten operations.

Procedural tasks are usually taught as a linear progression leading to a single top-level goal. There is usually little in the instructions that help to mentally organize the information for the learner, in the sense of providing an explanation or overview of the system or revealing how and where the procedure fits into a larger scheme. In other words, except for any intrinsic organization, or cuing built into the task, the learner may confront a situation that mainly demands rote memory.

Q. THE ROLE OF "THEORY" AND UNDERSTANDING

Recent research suggests that LTR can be improved by augmenting the teaching of procedural, complex rule-based and principle-based tasks with *qualitative explanations* or complementary/supplementary instructions designed to increase meaningfulness (Gentner, 1980, 1981; Smith and Goodman, 1982; Tourangeau and Sternberg, 1982; Kieras, 1981; Sturgis, Ellis, and Wulfeck, 1981). However, investigators differ in how they operationally define and test these kinds of elaborative instructions. "Qualitative explanations" really refer to what military training designers, managers, and instructors label as "theory." In deciding on the course content for subject matter which has a substantial theoretical foundation, e.g., basic electricity and electronics, there has long been serious controversy over what mixture of theory, facts, rules, concepts and principles to teach.

The appropriate answer to this psychological and educational question is, we believe, a complicated function of such factors as (a) the way that to-be-learned material will be used, and in what context; (b) how long it needs to be retained over periods of little or no practice; (c) whether it will need to be applied to (transferred to) another domain; (d) whether the difficulty of understanding the theory and using it to generate or regenerate correct performance is beyond the ability level of the trainee population; and (e) whether the K or S, *if not augmented by theory*, will constitute too formidable a memory burden (in view of the probable conditions and frequency of use). If we had the answers to this perplexing and pervasive question, we could resolve many of the crucial issues about the nature of, and relationships among learning, understanding, retention and transfer.

We are, however, making slow but steady progress towards being able to characterize tasks in terms of what kinds of qualitative explanations are most appropriate for promoting learning and retention. An operationally defined taxonomy of these types of explanations has been developed (Stevens and Steinberg, 1981; Smith and Goodman, 1982). It differentiates among linear, structural and functional explanations. *Linear* explanations are "bareboned", containing nothing more than an inventory of *what* to do -- essentially, what steps to follow, and in what order. *Structural* explanations tell the trainee *how* and/or *why* the various task or system components fit together, with the emphasis being on spatial relations. These explanations are static, and are often taught by using schematic diagrams. Konoske and Ellis (1985) selectively reviewed the recent literature dealing with the effectiveness of structural explanations on LTR of procedures and of conceptual information contained in expository prose. They conclude that successful structural instructions "should include spatial and component-part information...as well as...goal statements. In addition, structural information should be communicated using text, schematics, graphs and illustrations, whenever possible" (p. 13).

Functional explanations tell the learner about the cause-and-effect relationships among task components. Whereas structural explanations involve a static task, such as assembling a piece of equipment, functional explanations, in contrast, stress systems or situations which change over time, e.g., operating (as opposed to assembling or maintaining) equipment. Of particular interest is an experiment which provided subjects with a mental model of an unfamiliar device they had to learn to operate (Kieras and Bovair, 1984). The mental model was communicated, along with a functional explanation, by telling the experimental group that the control-panel device (that was the object of their learning) operated the phaser weapons on the starship Enterprise. A different group had to learn the procedures by rote, receiving no explanation of any sort. When tested one week after acquisition, the mental-model/functional-explanation group showed significantly better retention, including faster execution of the procedure, than the rote group. Kieras and Bovair concluded that the functional model proved superior because it was relevant to the actual task and made it possible to *infer* procedures which might not otherwise have been remembered.

The Kieras and Bovair conclusion reinforces a point we have emphasized before. Understanding of the *relationship* of parts to the whole; of *why* things must be done in a certain sequence and manner; of how and where the to-be-learned material *fits* within the learner's pre-existing K&S, is a powerful aid to LTR. Understanding enables the trainee to (a) furnish himself with cues to help retrieval; (b) recognize the relationship of externally provided or system-provided cues to the sought-for memory; and/or (c) rebuild or regenerate what was apparently forgotten by capitalizing on the conceptual/ideational scaffolding supplied by the understanding. Understanding also provides organizational coherence, thereby chunking and integrating the information into fewer KRRSs, and decreasing the memory burden.

Qualitative explanations for supplementary learning and understanding can be presented as analogies. These can be linear, structural or functional, and serve as a strategy for making new information fit better into an individual's KRRS network by relating the to-be-learned information to a similar body of knowledge or set of relationships which the learner *already* understands quite well. For example, Mayer (1975) used a linear and structural explanation of a computer in order to teach programming to his subjects. Learning and post-test performance were both improved.

In contrast, Riley (1983) used structural analogy to impart the conceptual understanding of how electrical circuits work. It was not sufficient, and she concluded that what was lacking was practice in using the analogy in the *context* of the task. What is needed, she maintained, is improved understanding of the kinds of qualitative mapping between tasks and analogies.

Qualitative explanations, whether direct or analogical, help the learner to construct mental models, which basically provide the learner with a more concrete, understandable

KRRS of the knowledge or skill in question. Mental models have been shown to improve learning and retention of complex tasks, both rule-based and principle-based (Gentner, 1980, 1981; Tourangeau and Sternberg, 1982; Kieras, 1981; Sturgis, Ellis and Wulfeck, 1981). Konoske and Ellis (1985), based on the different levels or purposes of qualitative explanations, have hypothesized the types of explanations that they believe facilitate the learning and retention of four different major kinds of procedural tasks. The following are representative examples of each of the procedural task categories displayed in the first column of the table: (a) Operation--driving a car; (b) Maintenance--tuning the engine of a car; (c) Paper-based tasks--completing a form for one's security clearance; and (d) Locating information or objects--using a reference manual or a dictionary.

Asterisk entries indicate that although the particular type of explanation shown can be, and usually is, used to teach the task in question, the type of explanation is not appropriate for facilitating either learning or retention. Taking the maintenance task as an example, we would not expect that a straightforward linear presentation of executable steps or sub-tasks would provide the needed information as to the way in which these steps relate to the functioning of items of equipment.

Table 2 is helpful because it tries to use cognitive-psychology concepts and theory to make specific directional predictions about whether a particular form of instructional strategy, *viz.*, qualitative explanations, will improve learning and retention.

We have no doubt that LTR can be improved significantly for all, except possibly very low-ability, learners, (no matter what the task) if the material to be learned is supplemented with appropriate understanding, meaningfulness, or elaborations designed to induce enhanced processing and thus result in qualitatively superior KRRSs. Instructional strategies that improve LTR can do so only by producing richer, more discriminable, more semantically or structurally differentiable, and/or more novel representations. It is, after all, how readily these encoded presentations can be accessed that determines the effectiveness of retrieval.

The practical problems of implementing the enhanced-processing, trace-enrichment approach to improving learning and LTR are not insurmountable, but they are severe. Promoting understanding or inducing enhanced encoding through semantic elaborations (such as the use of advanced organizers to provide a framework for meaningful internal organization) are believed to be the most effective techniques. Yet, for some people, for

TABLE 2**. TYPE OF PROCEDURAL TASK BY TYPE OF EXPLANATION

		Type of Explanation			
		Structural		Functional	
Type of Procedural Task	Linear	How	Why	How	Why
Operation	*	*	*	+	+
Maintenance					
Repair	*	+	+	+	+
Assembly	*	+	+	+	+
Paper-based					
Filling Forms	*	+			
Formatting Documents	*	+	+	+	
Locating Information/ Object	*	+	+	+	+

* Indicates that an explanation can be applied to the procedure, but is not expected to facilitate performance/retention.
**Reproduced from Konoske and Ellis, 1985, p. 21.
+ Indicates that applying the explanation to the procedure should facilitate performance/ retention.

NOTE: Explanations can be direct or analogical.

some tasks, expecially those requiring rote memorizing, even "semantically shallow" mnemonics can be very effective in increasing LTR (Bower, 1970, 1972).

Mnemonics (memory aids) can take the form of acronyms, visual imagery, and/or verbal mediators. Recently, the Western educational and psychological communities learned (Higbee and Kunihira, 1985) that a Japanese educator, M. Nakane, had developed a successful mnemonic system, based on verbal mediators, to aid in the learning and recall of "the orderly cognitive processes required in problem solving." (p. 58). Kilpatrick (1985), in commenting on Nakane's claims that his mnemonic system can *lead* to understanding, rejects the notion that "we can have doing before understanding and learning without understanding" (p. 65).

We believe that there are two important points which emerge from this ongoing argument about the value of mnemonic assists. The first is that the use of mnemonics is but one of many techniques designed to promote the formation of elaborate KRRSs. Yet, in spite of a considerable cognitively oriented resurgence of empirical research on this topic, we are still not appreciably closer to knowing when and how to use mnemonics in instruction.

The second point relates to the fundamental question of the role of theory that we just addressed. Nakane's claim that understanding will follow naturally from activities carried out without understanding is a highly controversial one. If true, it helps us to sidestep, in a pedagogical sense, the issue of how much theory to teach, since it asserts that understanding which was previously believed to be achieved only by a knowledge of theory can be achieved without teaching theory directly.

The major reviews that we charted (Table A-1) did not unearth very much research regarding the effects on LTR of what are typically regarded instructional-design or instructional-strategy variables. We have to turn to the prose- or text-learning literature to find any appreciable number of studies on these sorts of variables. Before we turn to that literature, we will discuss an experiment, using U.S. Army soliders, and dealing with a non-procedural, important military skill, that of visual aircraft recognition (Table B-7).

Baldwin, Cliborn and Foskett (1976) studied how ability levels influenced the training variable of self-paced vs. group-paced instruction. After dividing their subjects into groups of low, medium and high ability levels, they gave them all both kinds of instructional treatments. The low-ability group learned more under group-paced training than the intermediate-level soldiers. There was an interaction found between the training methods and the ability differences. For the self-paced condition, the medium-ability group showed superior skill acquisition as compared to the low-ability learners. For the high-ability groups, both training methods worked equally well.

Although the Baldwin et al. study did not test retention other than immediately after the acquisition trials, the authors contend that they can justifiably extrapolate their conclusions to LTR on the basis of data obtained by Vineberg (1975). Vineberg, whose study we will cover in a subsequent section on the individual-difference variable (see Table B-9), found retention differences in soldiers of different ability levels on Army basic-training tasks.

The variable of group-paced/self-paced training is a very important one. It lies at the heart of current controversies over the value and place of computer-based instruction (CBI), which embraces computer-assisted instruction (CAI), computer-managed instruction (CMI) and intelligent computer-assisted instruction (ICAI). For the most part, CBI is only as effective as the organization of content and the instructional strategies designed into any program.

The quality and effectiveness of CBI probably depends on how much we know (and can implement, via the power and flexibility of a computer) about managing the instructional-development process. As Montague and Wulfeck (1984) cogently point out, most currently available CBI provides training which could be provided without the medium of a computer. In this "mechanical page-turning" form, CBI, unsurprisingly, does not show any extra learning benefits as compared to more traditional, instructor-led training (except for student time saving in completing a course).

To the extent that recommendations we have made, and will make in a subsequent section, can be most economically, efficiently and flexibly implemented by on-line computerized training, we strongly support interactive CBI. It has unprecedented potential for inexpensively simulating, conceptually or in concrete detail, the actual operational environment, e.g., the military site or the industrial workplace. It can also easily serve the purpose of presenting, in readily understandable form, a pictorial or analogical representation of a complex or abstract set of rules, principles and relationships. This kind of mental-model representation is especially suitable when invisible processes have to be taught (Rigney and Lutz, 1974), since they can be animated and made observable and manipulable by the computer.

Because of its potential for increasing understanding, the computer should be able to bring about significantly improved LTR. It is tempting to believe that the computer, because of its great technological *potential*, can solve the problems of so much ineffective instruction. However, we echo the belief of Montague and Wulfeck (1984), that the prospects for substantial improvements in the quality and memorability of instruction depend, first, on achieving a better understanding of the instructional process (aided by evolving research in cognitive science); and, second, on the use of powerful programming capabilities to produce interactive instruction suggested by the research.

R. RELATIONSHIP OF PROSE LEARNING TO REAL-WORLD TASKS

Earlier, we indicated that the literature on prose/text learning was a relatively fertile source of research on the role of instructional manipulations or conditions on LTR. Although prose learning, upon first consideration, may not seem to be too applicable to military or other real-life training issues, we can find good reasons to focus on the text-learning literature. For the most part, prose learning is what one achieves from reading -- usually stories or narrative material, or expository material of the kind found in school books. What makes these kinds of prose similar to each other is that they are all composed of connected (and therefore organized and cohesive) material. In the same way, procedures too are characterized by the fact that their steps or subtasks are held together by a common thread based on the overlying top-down goal of getting the procedural task, as a whole, executed successfully. Continuous motor-control tasks, we have seen earlier in this paper, represent the category most resistant to decay over the long term -- because their inherent continuity means cohesion, and cohesion makes for the kind of task organization which promotes memorability. Our point here is that we have just named three major varieties of tasks that have almost always been separately studied because they are viewed as representing taxonomically different categories. Yet, from the standpoint of memorability, it would seem that they have much in common. It would further follow that the Army's UDA approach (of predicting decay for procedural tasks based mainly on major organizational characteristics) might well be adaptable to prose learning and continuous-control motor learning.

Studying the learning and retention of prose is also important because we get much of our needed information, especially of the technical and scientific variety, from the printed word. And the majority of school subjects depend heavily on conveying information through reading. In addition, the kind of knowledge we acquire from reading prose serves as the underpinnings for later, more advanced learning; for understanding of difficult, abstract concepts; for generalization and positive transfer; and for decision making and problem solving.

Some cognitive psychologists studying prose learning have focussed on memory for routine events, suggesting two ways in which such events might be organized. Schank and Abelson's (1977) script theory emphasized the temporal sequence of events. In contrast, research on story organization has emphasized the hierarchical structure or centrality of events. Although Galambos and Rips (1982) discuss these two different organizing frameworks, what they call "routines" are essentially procedures, and what they call "episodes" are the subtasks or steps of a procedure. These terms are used to provide a vocabulary compatible with that used by schema theorists in discussing memory.

"Essentially, routines are the types of activities that Schank and Abelson's (1977) script theory was intended to capture" (Galambos & Rips, 1982, p. 261). Examples of routines that are given range from the relatively tightly-structured type (changing a tire) to the more fluid routine of "going to the movies." After comparing the effect of sequence information vs. centrality information in terms of memorability, Galambos & Rips (1982) conclude that both information sources "may be computed as needed, rather than precompiled" (p. 260).

S. INSTRUCTIONAL STRATEGIES FOR PROSE LEARNING AND RETENTION

When a task to be learned is not intrinsically comprised of organizationally continuous or coherent elements, subtasks, steps or episodes, then the attibutes of organization, meaningfulness, or novelty can be *imposed* to provide greater memorial durability. There are a good number of factors that can be varied to increase prose-passage organization. Probably the one most studied and conceptually heuristic is that of advance organizers. Ausubel (1960), who popularized the concept, maintained that presenting information (such as a topical heading or superordinate statement) to the learner before a learning event will improve retention by providing an anchoring idea into which the more detailed information in the passage can fit.

The literature on the effect of advance organizers is mainly focused on acquisition, and is not at all conclusive. Barnes and Clawson (1975), in reviewing 32 studies in that literature, concluded: "Advance organizers, as presently constructed, do not facilitate learning" (p. 651). However, Mayer (1979) claims that the Barnes and Clawson review was flawed; he presented contrary evidence based on experiments which overcame the limitations of the Barnes and Clawson review. Mayer's conclusion was that "there are definable situations in which advance organizers result in broader learning outcomes" (p. 381). He clarified "broader learning outcomes" when he stated that organizing aids "seem to have their strongest positive effects not on measures of retention, but rather on measures of transfer" (p. 382).

Unfortunately, as Mayer acknowledges, there is no reliable formula for creating effective organizers. Yet, he suggests four factors as prescriptive criteria for facilitative advance organizers:

1. The organizer should help the learner to generate the logical relationships in the to-be-learned material.

2. It should assist in relating unfamiliar material to one's world knowledge.

3. It should be easy for the learner to acquire and use.

4. It should be supplied in situations where, say, due to inexperience or stress, the learner would not be likely to supply his own organizing framework.

E. Gagne (1978), in reviewing the long-term retention of prose material, interprets the effect of advance organizers in terms of J. Anderson's (1976) "ACT" model or theory. Although Anderson (1982) has updated his theory since Gagne's review, her application of Anderson's basically associationistic model seems plausible and convincing. The Anderson model, like the more cognitive views of Kintsch (1974) and Norman and Bobrow (1976), essentially postulates the existence of KRRSs (which are referred to as schemata), a primary function of which is to determine how information being acquired should be analyzed and processed. Qualitative errors made in retention tests conform to these general schemata, strongly supporting the view that memory is, in part, reconstructive.

It is not feasible, nor intended, in this review, to cover all the hundreds of research articles dealing with instructional variables that affect the acquisition and LTR of prose. Both Shimmerlik (1978) and E. Gagne (1978) review that literature from somewhat different vantage points. Shimmerlik focuses on the role of organizational factors in memory. Most of the studies she reviews follow the list-learning approach, which is dominated by the use of free recall. She points out that this paradigm, characterized by the absence of externally provided cues, yields "the most striking effects of organization" (p. 117). Organization has "increasing influence as the burden of retrieval rests increasingly upon the learner" (p. 117). After acknowledging that free recall is not generally tapped by classroom tests, she contends that education should strive to ensure that information in memory is available to the learner in a variety of situations, not merely when cued by a test item. She argues for research to identify the conditions under which both cue-dependent and trace-dependent forgetting occur, as well as the types of cues which promote retention following different learning conditions. Such results might reveal ways to minimize cue-dependent forgetting by having students learn how to use cues themselves.

E. Gagne (1978) reviewed the then-recent research on long-term prose retention by grouping the material into four phases: prelearning history, the events taking place just prior to the reading task, the actual reading per se, and a retention period. Table C-1 is our attempt to represent some of the most typical instructional variables used in prose learning, extracted from Gagne's review. We have provided a strength-of-effect rating, based on the criteria we used for the same kind of judgment we expressed in Tables A-2 through A-7. Individual differences in prior knowledge and learner abilities, which are shown as rows 1.A. and 1.B., correspond to the stage that Gagne calls "prelearning history."

The reader should observe that almost all of the beneficial effects attributable to the instructional variables shown can be interpreted in terms of meaningful organization or enhanced processing -- supporting the position we have taken consistently throughout this paper.

During each of the phases she identified, Gagne believes, manipulations can be performed which will "alter the cognitive structure in any of three ways" (p. 638):

1. The manipulations might increase the number of pathways emerging from nodes activated by a probe stimulus. Variables that might exert this effect

include the extent of the learner's existing related knowledge, the type of elaborations he usually employs on his own (e.g., creating a bizarre image), advance organizers, the relevance of the information, and the review of notes.

2. The manipulations may "increase the strength of a particular pathway" (p. 638). Relevant variables here include prequestions that promote rehearsal, directions to rehearse, interspersed questions, postquestions, and repetition of the information after the reading has occurred.

3. The manipulations may increase the number of routes leading to the information to be retained. Doing so increases the potential for unwanted interference as well as for positive transfer. A variable that could exert this effect is that of reading "competing" information just before or after reading the passage to be learned and remembered.

Based on her review, E. Gagne (1978) identifies four instructional strategies that seem to be most promising from a practical standpoint: (a) remind the learners of related knowledge they already possess; (b) teach them various ways to provide their own elaborations, such as mnemonics; (c) be sure that the instruction makes repeated use of the information presented; and (d) during the retention interval, provide for and encourage the elaboration of the material acquired.

At several places in this paper, we have discussed the major theoretical issue of whether we learn mainly by strengthening connections, by increasing the quality of the associated components, and/or by increasing the number of the encoded associations. As just noted, E. Gagne (1978) contends that increasing the strength of a particular associative pathway is one way in which retention can be facilitated. We have taken the view that all of these mechanisms can, and usually do, operate simultaneously as we learn and commit to memory.

The concept of level of processing was discussed earlier in connection with the degree of original learning. When the literature talks about elaboration as a strategy for improving learning and memory, it is referring to how much and what kind of processing is occurring.

Anderson and Reder (1979) contend that the main significance of deeper processing for retention is that it affects primarily the *number* of elaborations produced by learners, and that these elaborations establish more redundant encodings of the information being learned. The extent of elaboration, these investigators assert, is what is critical, especially to promote LTR. They argue that the depth- or breadth-of-processing phenomenon is as important to prose material as it is to the more artificial verbal learning material of the pre-cognitive experimental psychology laboratory.

Other investigators have also tried to explain why and how the depth/breadth-of-processing construct operates to enhance memory; they postulate that the depth to which the item is processed yields different types or strengths of traces (Craik & Lockhart, 1972; Craik & Tulving, 1975; Kintsch, 1975; and Wickelgren, 1973). For example, Kintsch (1975) suggests that traces of propositional knowledge decay at a slower rate than do traces of lexical knowledge. Wickelgren (1973) had also maintained that propositional traces decay less quickly, but he attributed the cause to less interference from other memory traces.

Although Anderson and Reder acknowledge some role for the type (i.e., the quality) of the elaborated product, they argue that the most critical determinant in successfully predicting recall is the "quantity" of elaborations. On the other hand, they claim that manipulating "quality," while holding quantity constant, should not be as good a predictor. However, although Anderson and Reder downgrade the role of quality of knowledge representation in determining the decay propensity, we believe, as we have stressed previously on several occasions, that the quality of the KRRS is an essential concept for explaining why certain kinds of elaborations work better than others, and for explaining the effects of elaboration on increasing the likelihood of interference and positive transfer. We see no way in which the number of elaborations could principally determine the probability of transfer. We can hypothesize a situation in which two learners generate an equal number of elaborations. The first learner's elaborations are all minor semantic and conceptual variations on the same theme. In contrast, the second learner's elaboration encompass many more and diverse domains and concepts. We would expect the second learner to show better LTR and far better facilitative transfer.

T. VARIABLE: THE RETENTION INTERVAL/REFRESHER TRAINING

The conclusion that emerges most clearly from Table A-5 is that, as the retention period gets longer without use of the learned skill or knowledge, decay tends to increase. As Schendel, Shields and Katz (1978) observe, there is a classic curve of forgetting: the absolute amount of decay increases with time, whereas the apparent rate of forgetting declines over time. However, from our prior discussions of other variables, it is evident that the amount of forgetting during the retention interval is very sensitive to the type of task, the level of original learning, and the conditions and strategies of instruction. For example, a continuous motor task will be more resistant to decay, over any time period, than a rote memory task. Similarly, a highly overlearned skill will be retained longer than a barely mastered one. Although these conclusions may seem banal and obvious, they represent essentially all we know about how the length of the retention period affects long-term memory.

Part of the conceptual problem in examining the influence of the retention interval lies in its arbitrary nature. As we stressed previously, the end of acquisition (which signals the beginning of the retention period) is itself at times a somewhat capricious point on the learning curve. To speak really meaningfully about the retention period, one has to consider whether attempts during that interval to practice, rehearse, or relearn exhibit different properties than the same mental operations performed during the acquisition phase. We are really asking the question: is learning in its early stages different (taking a qualitative, process-oriented perspective) from learning in its later stages? Certainly, for example, learning that involves the development of insights can be very much different, as Lane (in press) points out, than learning, say, a vocabulary list in a foreign-language course. Put another way, we can compare two hypothetical learners involved with identical learning tasks. Learner A has learned 50% of the target mastery criterion. Learner B had originally learned 100%, i.e., met the mastery criterion, but over the course of a nine-month nonuse interval, had forgotten 50% of what he had acquired. Is the information or skill that Learner B forgot the same as that which Learner A has *yet* to learn?

We can find no empirical studies that speak directly to this kind of question. We have already supplied evidence that supports the claim that specific components of what has been learned decay at different rates, largely as a function of each component's intrinsic memorability and cohesion with other task components. There is also evidence that the

89

kind of retention measure used (a variable that we take up in the next section) can strongly influence what seems to have been forgotten. For example, McGeoch (1932) compared nonsense syllable learning with maze (motor) learning. When retention was measured by the number of trials saved in relearning the tasks, the nonsense syllables were better remembered. However, the difference between the two tasks turned out to be insignificant when error scores were used. Gardlin and Sitterley (1972) observe that, for procedural tasks, errors of commission are most susceptible to prolonging the retention period.

U. REFRESHER-TRAINING APPROACHES

The point we have been trying to build up to is that the practice/refresher-training needs of the individual who had once acquired the K or S, but has since experienced some forgetting, seem to be different from the needs of the new learner. The former individual (whom we will refer to, for convenience, as the *retrainee*) probably has a different perspective on what he once knew, a sort of top-down view gained by once having performed the entire task successfully. The beginning trainee, on the other hand, must necessarily have a much more limited perspective while he is learning -- a bottom-up view -- especially if the task is hierarchical and/or complex.

When it is known in advance that there will be an appreciable period of little or no use of a learned K or S, it seems most desirable that enough practice or rehearsal be provided, with the proper frequency and spacing, so as to prevent an unacceptable amount of decay from occurring. If this is not possible, then actual refresher training needs to be carried out before performance deteriorates below an acceptable level. We have previously discussed several approaches for predicting [based either on first-trial acquisition data (Rigg, 1983) or task-attribute data (Rose et al., 1984)] how much decay would occur over given periods of nonuse. We have also described Bahrick's (1979) prescription that, for effective maintenance of knowledge, practice should be spaced at intervals about the same length as the decay interval separating practice from test.

Providing effective practice, or formal, scheduled refresher training obviously requires time and specialized resources. Given that we have some idea, based upon the prediction techniques just noted, of when practice, rehearsal or retraining is in order, we need some relatively quick, inexpensive way to overcome the decay. The literature here holds out some promise. Annett (1979) contends that different kinds of rehearsal, including imaginary (covert) practice and symbolic rehearsal, can be effective. Naylor and Briggs (1961) point out that the relative efficiency of real and imaginary practice varies with the task and with the degree of symbolic rehearsal. However, because covert rehearsal can retard forgetting, Naylor and Briggs suggest that the fidelity of simulation need not be as high for refresher training.

Our point about the different perspectives between a beginning trainee and a retrainee becomes quite relevant here. The latter should be able to re-achieve his original mastery level with selected part-task training, and/or conceptual simulation (Stevens & Steinberg, 1981; Young, 1983; Hutchins, Hollan & Norman, 1985). Cognitive theory informs us that an entire network of KRRSs can be accessed and restimulated if a conceptually important cue is provided in an appropriate context.

Other partial or brief cuing situations also can retard decay or facilitate relearning. Hurlock and Montague (see Table A-6) conclude that procedural skills can be quickly reacquired by studying written job aids or reminder material such as technical manuals. Furthermore, the information provided and/or practice afforded by taking a test (especially if it is a hands-on type) can also serve to provide refresher training.

V. VARIABLE: METHODS OF TESTING RETENTION/CONDITIONS OF RECALL

We have already covered a great deal of what would ordinarily be discussed under this heading. We had to do so in order to explain why it was often so difficult and confusing to compare the strengths of effect, for any given variables, across different experiments. It should have become clear then that it is inappropriate to trust conclusions based upon different measures of retention, e.g., recognition, free recall and relearning. We will, therefore, limit this section to a brief review of the main findings about the major techniques for assessing retention, and about the relationship of the recall context to the context present during original learning.

In recognition of the different results obtainable from the various methods of retention used, Naylor and Briggs (1961) [see Table A-6] wisely advise using, as the retention measure, the one that is "important in the operational task" (p. 26).

Hurlock and Montague (1982) join Naylor and Briggs (1961) in concluding that retention can be aided by increasing the perceived similarity between the conditions or context of the recall situation and those of original learning. We believe that this empirically-supported conclusion also happens to represent sound theoretical reasoning. The similarity across the learning and retention environments allows the stimuli of the latter to serve as richer memory-retrieval cues. At the same time, cue conflict is decreased, and interference is thereby lessened.

We previously discussed the fact that there is no predictive relationship between relearning and a recognition or recall test. In other words, trainees who might show a 50% or more level of decay, as measured by free recall, might be able to relearn the task in 2 trials. If the original learning of the task had taken 20 trials, quite a substantial savings score is obtained, especially in comparison with the poor recall score.

The empirical findings from the literature on motor memory tells us that the relearning of motor skills frequently yields a savings score ranging from 50% (Schendel, Shields & Katz, 1978) to 90% after as much as a 22-month interval (Annett, 1979). These findings provide a clue about why relearning can occur so rapidly even though other retention measures indicate marked forgetting.

We can find nothing in the literature that attempts to confront theoretically this apparent paradox. We suggest that the relearning-method advantage of motor skills is in large part due to the nature of the task. A motor task, especially of a continuous control nature, has a good deal of integrative cohesiveness. It cannot be divided up into definable, separable units that correspond, say, to the steps of a procedure. It cannot therefore be easily tested for retention by asking the individual to recall or recognize it. Rather, he must perform it in a hands-on way to demonstrate his remaining proficiency. Thefefore the savings score, based on the relearning paradigm, is logically the retention method of choice and, in fact, has been the one most used for assessing motor memory (Annett, 1979).

What might be happening as an individual sets about relearning a motor skill he had once mastered but has now partially forgotten? We would posit two facilitative influences:

1. By the very act of reproducing some of the learned motor behavior, the individual *generates his own cues* which serve to trigger some of the remainder of the learned behaviors associated with that skill. In turn, the newly reproduced actions provide

cues which reactivate still more of the motor skill. This cycle continues until the skill is completely relearned.

2. In the usual setting and circumstances called for by the paradigm of relearning, the individual himself, in effect, *re-creates* the context of his original learning because he goes through the same steps and behaviors that he performed earlier. This correspondence of actions provides an associative link across the learning and retention environments. As we pointed out above, similarity between these two environments has proven effective in promoting durable retention.

W. VARIABLE: INDIVIDUAL DIFFERENCES

Individual differences, as used in the learning and memory literature, most often apply to differences in abilities, usually the broad ability known as general intelligence. However, other individual-differences variables have occasionally been manipulated. These include prior achievement, motivation, hypnosis and the effects of aging. Table A-7 reflects the influence of some of these variables, but their strength-of-effect rating is not high enough to allow us to make reliable statements about the nature and magnitude of their impact. Hypnosis, for example, is still an unpredictable variable, and it is impractical, scientifically and politically, to consider seriously for mass training purposes.

What does emerge most strongly from Table A-7 is the explanation (Hurlock & Montague, 1982; Schendel, Shields & Katz, 1978; Hagman & Rose, 1983) for why ability differences can substantially affect retention. All these authors conclude that higher-ability learners tend to achieve higher levels of learning than less able individuals. Therefore, when decay occurs, the more able learners will maintain their learning advantage. However, as Hurlock and Montague clearly recognize, there should be no retention differences between the differing-ability groups if they both have learned to the same mastery criterion.

In our previous discussions of overlearning, we presented various viewpoints (e.g., Loftus, 1985) which discussed the relationship between the degree of OL and the rate and amount of decay. This relationship is probably far from a simple one. For example, people may differ markedly with respect to the nature and quality of learning strategies they employ. Those that they select and can use effectively are a function, in part, of individual

93

differences in prior achievement, training expectations, initial skill level, motivation, cognitive style and, of course, ability and aptitudes. The efficiency and speed with which they reach any given mastery criterion may well be principally determined by one or more individual-difference variables. And the degree to which any particular individual-difference variable is mobilized and, in turn, induces an effective learning strategy, is largely a function of the demands of the learning task and conditions.

If what needs to be learned, for example, is a complex domain (e.g., physics), composed of a blend of facts, rules, principles, relationships and concepts, it is unreasonable to believe that the more able learner will not employ a larger number of more effective strategies than the lower-ability individual. Different strategies result in the various parts of a complex task or domain being learned to differing degrees of strength, quality, understanding and transfer potential. Consequently, it follows that there will be differing rates of decay of the diverse components constituting the learned domain.

We believe that we have shown logically that differential decay rates for the components of a complex domain can be causally related to learning strategies governed by individual differences. A real-world, empirical study (Hall, Ford, Whitten, & Plyant, 1983) of a similar complex domain provides independent support for our position. As can be seen in Table B-8, U.S. Navy sailors who had completed a self-paced, CMI course in basic electricity and electronics (BE/E) were tested on the two phases they had mastered: Direct-Current (DC) theory, and Alternating-Current (AC) theory. The latter is typically more difficult to learn. When tested after 18 to 34 days of nonuse, the higher-ability sailors (based upon scores in military tests which tapped general intellectual ability) forgot significantly less than the lower-ability trainees. Furthermore, a significantly greater proportion of decay was found for AC theory than for DC theory. The fact that this learning was accomplished in a self-paced course ensured that all trainees learned to the same mastery criteria, although the more able individuals were able to reach criterion more quickly.

In contrast to the Hall et al. (1983) study, Vineberg (1975) [Table B-9] studied the retention of U.S. Army basic-training tasks (mostly procedural and non-complex) after a nonuse period of 6 weeks. The soldiers used were grouped by mental-ability categories II, III, and IV, with category II being more able, and category IV less able. These ability

94

levels were operationalized by scores on the same kind of military test that Hall et al. had used.

Vineberg attributed his retention results to the different levels of OL reached by the three groups: the more able learners retained proportionally more than the moderate- and low-ability individuals over the same retention period. Vineberg concluded that his obtained retention differences might have been reduced if all of his trainees had learned to a common mastery level. However, as we have pointed out, because his conclusions are based on relatively simple procedural tasks, they do not necessarily apply to other kinds of tasks, especially those demanding a high level and quality of processing operations.

So far in this section we have emphasized the role that individual differences can play in affecting the acquisition phase directly, and the retention phase indirectly, i.e., via the product of the acquisition process. However, as we have discussed at some length previously, there are learning strategies which not only aid in acquisition, but also result in the kind of enhanced processing that increases the memorability of the acquired K or S. Those learners whose abilities, aptitudes, past experience, etc. have equipped them with a larger and more varied repertoire of memory-enhancing strategies should retain more information for longer periods. Interestingly, Anderson and Reder (1979) report (based on a 1976 personal communication from J.R. Hayes) what seem to be enduring individual differences in the tendency and ability to elaborate historical facts. On the basis of a pretest of their memory for historical facts, individuals were classified as those who recall historical facts well and those who do not. When given a fictitious history passage to read, the former group was superior on a test of the facts it contained. When this group was asked to free-recall the passage, they generated many elaborations that were not given. These elaborations were more than mere paraphrases of the passage or simple inferences.

In contrast, the group characterized by poor memory for history offered very few elaborations. The logical conclusion is that the enhancement added by the elaborations facilitated retention. But the question that these results suggest is theoretically fascinating: Is there a specific tendency and/or "ability" to produce memory-promoting elaborations for (a) historical facts; (b) facts in general; and/or (c) any kind of material to be learned and retained that can benefit from such embellishment?

To the extent that the memory process is *reconstructive*, rather than merely *reproductive*, there is opportunity for strategies that aid in locating and identifying a trace to be applied at the point of retrieval. The more complex, meaningful and difficult is the domain that has been learned, the more the retrieval operation may resemble that of problem solving (Williams & Hollan, 1981; Norman & Bobrow, 1979). Strategic approaches to successful problem solving can be extremely varied, and the strategies that are invoked are likely to be a product in large part of individual differences, particularly in ability and cognitive style. Cognitive style refers to an individual's preferred and consistent way of organizing information and translating the processed information into expression. Each cognitive style possesses an "associated strategy for problem solving" (Modrick, Levitt, Alden & Henke, 1975). Battig (1979) asserts that learners show wide variability in processing techniques "even when a single fixed optimal strategy may appear quite sufficient for successful performance" (p. 28). He then adds that any memory experiment "most likely represents a kind of problem-solving task" (p. 28) to the typical individual subject.

The fact that individual differences are many and varied, and can substantially influence learning and retention is a critical consideration for those charged with designing and managing instruction. The lock-step, instructor-dominated approach to the delivery of training and education does not capitalize on each learner's particular strengths, nor avoid his weaknesses. Ideally, self-paced, individualized instruction should be able to take full advantage of each trainee's unique cognitive abilities and non-cognitive attributes. One particular promising approach which may be cost effective is that of learner control. Here the technique is to train the learner to make his own decisions about which strategies best fit the ongoing learning demands (Merrill, 1975, 1980; Reigeluth, 1979).

For the full potential of individual differences to be realized in instruction, we need much more reliable information about how abilities and aptitudes interact with instructional treatments -- the so-called ATI (aptitude-treatment interaction). "Actually, all attempts at individualizing instruction rest explicitly or implicitly on hypothesized interactions between some aptitude and treatment variables, but most work on adaptive instruction has failed to formulate such hypotheses explicitly or to study them directly" (Snow, 1980, p. 1). ATI can serve as the basis for assigning trainees to differing instructional treatments, thereby providing what Snow (1980) has called "a kind of 'macroadaptation' of instruction" (p. 1). On the other hand, ATI can be used to inform and evaluate "microadaptive" approaches such as those used in CAI.

VIII. CONCLUSIONS

Unlike some reviews which save their own interpretations and conclusions until after presenting all the data, we have discussed our views in detail, offered our own theory-oriented explanations, and suggested practical educational implications throughout this paper. As a result, there is no need now to provide an extensive set of duplicative conclusions and recommendations. We will introduce this section by briefly recapitulating the essence of the cognitive-psychology perspective, which has provided us with the framework for a revised interpretation of much of the literature on LTR. After noting the essential implications of the cognitive-processing viewpoint for instruction, we will offer a selected set of conclusions, chosen because of their broad scope and generality.

INSTRUCTIONAL IMPLICATIONS

Cognitive psychology sees the learner as an active organism who processes information by organizing it, elaborating it and encoding it into a representational state or trace suitable for storage over extended time intervals. All information taken in is related to prior knowledge, and represented in memory as schemata [or what we have termed knowledge-representation retrieval structures (KRRS)]. When instructors or books or other delivery media dispense material to be learned, the learning does not occur automatically. Quite the contrary, the acquisition is a constructive, deliberative process which is significantly affected by such interacting factors as (a) the trainee's world knowledge; (b) his ability and tendency to use information-processing strategies for learning and remembering; and (c) the nature (complexity and difficulty) of the task and conditions of learning.

The role and responsibilities of the instructor must be reconsidered. The teacher (or the automatic, possibly computer-based program) should strive to facilitate the learner's construction of meaning and the processing of information to make it more manageable, understandable, and memorable. Instructors should maintain attention and promote both

97

learning and durable memory by (a) using questions and instructional objectives; (b) encouraging learners to relate relevant KRRSs to the information to be learned; (c) explaining the nature and workings of various learning strategies (e.g., analogies and mnemonic aids) which promote both understanding and LTR. In short, according to the cognitive framework, the instructor does not just deliver information to the learner in the traditional sense. Rather, he designs, conducts and monitors the educational activities that promote the learner's active construction of verbal and imaginal cognitive processes that make sense out of new information by relating it to current knowledge.

1.   Learning/Training Conditions

a.   The greater the degree to which the learner has mastered the K or S, the slower will be the rate of decay. This degree of learning or mastery is usually increased by having the learner gain more practice with the material (overlearning). It can also be increased by inducing the trainee to more deeply and extensively process the material, e.g., in order to overcome interference.

b.   The "quality" (as contrasted to the "strength") of the memory traces formed while learning is probably the single most important determinant of LTR, especially for complex and/or difficult tasks. This quality is a function of the degree and kind of cognitive processing performed on the TBL material. It can be increased through instructional design and strategies.

c.   LTR will increase the more that the context of the training environment and conditions of training resemble those of the job or real-world environment in which the learned K or S will be applied.

d.   The more that the learner can meaningfully integrate new incoming information with his existing knowledge structures, the better the new information will be remembered. Maximal integration that will most benefit acquisition, transfer and LTR occurs when the new information is understood in terms of what the learner *already* comprehends, i.e., in terms of existing "mental models" relating to the same or a similar domain.

e.   Since memory is largely reconstructive we should, wherever applicable, teach concepts, principles and rules to complement or supplement teaching rote knowledge or facts. This will promote effective understanding of a task domain and thus allow the learner to later generate or regenerate details which would not otherwise be available to memory. This understanding also acts as an integrating, cohesive framework which distinguishes this task from others in memory, and serves to better cue within-task steps or components.

2. Characteristics of the Task

a. Certain attributes of a task which essentially represent its complexity and "difficulty" can be analyzed to yield a kind of task-characteristic memorability measure. This measure can be successfully used, particularly for procedural tasks, to predict how much the task will decay over any given interval of nonuse.

b. Different components (subtasks, steps) of a complex task (defined generally as a task which may tap different abilities, require reasoning or problem solving, and/or contain multiple, interrelated facts or concepts) will decay over time at different rates. Attempts to assign these kinds of tasks a single, robust decay-rate predictor would seem fruitless.

c. In learning from prose or text, different kinds of information (e.g., paragraph theme, sentence gist and sentence wording) yield different retention curves. These findings could stem from different kinds and degrees of processing of these different attributes.

d. Skills (such as typing or reading), which have become more highly organized, cohesive, proceduralized or automated through extensive practice, show negligible decay over long periods of nonuse.

3. Predicting the Course of Retention During Nonuse Intervals

a. The approximate rate of decay can be predicted for certain kinds of tasks (typically procedural in nature) whose components are organizationally related to each other and the total task in a relatively straightforward manner. [As noted earlier, the Army Research Institute (Rose et al., 1985) has developed and successfully used an algorithm which combines raters' judgements of the individual memorability of a task's characteristics. This leads to a "projected rate of proficiency loss."]

b. Two Army-sponsored studies (Rigg & Gray, 1981; Rigg, 1983) report that they have successfully used an algorithm, based on mathematical learning theory, to predict the percent of military procedural task decay over given periods of time. The input data for the algorithm come from the individual's performance on his first learning trial.

(Unfortunately, the available reports on this work do not provide enough supporting data and source verification for us to provide the reader with a credible analysis and evaluation of this technique.)

IX. RECOMMENDATIONS FOR INCREASING LTR

Although there is necessarily some overlap with the Conclusions we have presented above, this section attempts to summarize, briefly, actual steps that can be taken either to directly promote LTR by some training intervention, or slow down the rate of decay by intervention during the nonuse retention period.

A. TRAINING TASK ANALYSIS

1. A training task analysis (performed to aid in designing an instructional system) should carefully consider the recall context (the operational or real-world environment in which the learner must function) and the possible cuing stimuli that may be present.

2. The training task analysis should rate the memorability of the various task characteristics (see Item 3a above under "Predicting the Course of Retention During Nonuse Intervals" for a metric which might be applied). With these measures, it might be possible to selectively "overtrain" the less memorable attributes so that their specific retention curves could be improved.

B. INSTRUCTIONAL STRATEGIES/CONDITIONS OF LEARNING

1. Design instruction which causes the learner to *process* the material to be learned at an *enhanced* level. This typically involves providing him with elaborative associations, advance organizers, topical headings, and the like. Enhanced processing, when appropriate to the content and expected cuing conditions and context of the recall situation, will result in more discriminable and retrievable memory traces.

2. Wherever possible, if concepts and relationships are part of what is to be learned, then directly teach and test *understanding*, as contrasted to any rote-memory components. The understanding (a) provides a meaningful ideational scaffolding to hold together and cue the components; and (b) facilitates positive transfer.

3. For critical tasks where it is especially important that performance be errorless, stable and durable, "overtrain" the learners by increasing the required mastery-criterion level, or by inducing the learner to process the material both more intensively and extensively. This can be done by a variety of methods. Examples include requiring the trainee to overcome deliberately introduced interference, or to work with degraded or incomplete learning material.

4. For tasks (such as procedures) which mainly involve discrete component steps that flow sequentially, add elaborative verbal linking associations to each step which does not provide intrinsic cuing to its immediately following step. This will serve as a memory assist for recalling the correct procedural order, which is one of the main kinds of errors found for the retention of procedural tasks.

5. Where unrelated facts or rote material are to be learned, mnemonic devices, such as acronyms or unusual imaginal associations, can be inserted to aid the learner to create a more distinctive and, hence, more accessible trace. The distinctiveness or increased identifiability of the trace also reduces interference due to similarity.

6. Allow the higher-ability learners to set their own pace, but provide them with relatively well-designed material structured to promote enhanced processing and, consequently, more durable memory. We are thus recommending individualized instruction in the sense of pace, but not in the sense of choosing one's own path through the course of learning.

C. COUNTERACTING MEMORY DECAY DURING NONUSE PERIODS

1. "Imaginary" or covert rehearsal can prove effective in retarding decay. Thus during periods of nonuse, have the trainee mentally rehearse or act out the skill or the knowledge learned.

2. In dealing with a simple, or a well-organized complex task, we need to provide only occasional practice and short periods of rehearsal to sustain the task or skill. Even practicing one central aspect of the total task will be useful in retarding further delay of the rest of the task. This has particular significance for the use of part-task simulators to provide more limited and cheaper training.

3. Procedural skills can be quickly relearned, without actually having to execute the procedure, by studying printed jobs aids or reminder material such as technical manuals.

4. A low-cost equivalent of refresher training can be provided by *testing* the learner, especially using tests of the hands-on, performance-type when applicable. An added benefit is that the test results can be used for diagnostic and evaluative purposes.

D. FIDELITY OF SIMULATION

1. Where complex, abstract relationships among systems, functions, phenomena, equipment, etc., must be taught, there need be only that degree of simulation of the physical system and its parts sufficient to induce mental representations of the relationships. The fidelilty required for this *conceptual* simulation can be much lower than for full-scale dynamic simulation, especially if the simulation permits online direct manipulation by the learner of a computer-controlled instructional interface. (An example of this is the Navy's STEAMER (Stevens & Steinberg, 1981) intelligent training system, for teaching the operation and maintenance of a steam plant.)

2. As noted above, in item 2 of "Counteracting Memory Decay During Nonuse Periods," practice on even one aspect or part of a task can be potent enough to *reinstate* the entire task. Existing part-task simulators therefore might be used effectively to provide this practice.

X. ISSUES FOR FURTHER RESEARCH AND DEVELOPMENT

In view of the compelling importance of the long-term retention problem, we identify a number of areas and issues which deserve further research and development. These range from theory-building and hypotheses-testing to practical, applied, quite focussed research. The descriptions below cover those areas and issues we consider most important. They start with the more basic-research concerns and end with the more applied concerns.

1. How "motor memory" is represented in trace form.

2. The relationship of individual differences to LTR.

3. A more precise, preferably objectively or operationally measurable, index of "how much" learning has taken place. This will, among other things, allow us to compare across individuals, and to have a common point from which to measure the course of retention.

4. What are the *qualitative* effects of overlearning for different kinds of complex tasks? This relates to the fundamental question of whether sheer repetition, as opposed to strategic cognitive processing, promotes more durable memory.

5. (Related to the prior item.) How do we measure the quality of what one has learned as opposed to the amount or magnitude? (We know that, as one learns complex, meaningful material, the abilities required change, insight occurs, understanding develops, etc.) The "quality" index may well be more predictive of LTR and facilitative transfer than any quantitative measure.

6. (Related to the prior two items.) We need operational definitions (supported by empirical evidence) of the "distinctiveness" or the "discriminability" of memory traces. This knowledge is essential if we are to develop a prescriptive science of instruction.

These characteristics of traces have been conclusively associated with increased memorability.

7. How do we definably and reliably increase the degree or level of original learning (and thereby improve LTR) without having to increase the time spent in the acquisition phase? This relates to a very practical concern: At what price can we demand a more stringent mastery criterion?

8. In organizing instruction so as to achieve enhanced processing and the resultant improved memorability, is it more effective to encourage the learner to form his *own* enriched memory encodings, or to provide him with all of the elaborative material?

9. We need an operational definition of task complexity that will inform us of the memorability of the total task, as well as its components taken individually. We further require a means for deriving an index, preferably a quantitative one, that we can effectively use for twin purposes:

(a) for determining the ease of learning the task; and

(b) for predicting the decay rate of the task or any of its major components.

10. There is some evidence that the instructional needs for relearning (refresher training) are different than those for original learning. To what extent, and how, can we "abbreviate" or "streamline" the degree and kind of instruction needed for refresher training?

11. We need to develop a model, algorithm or equation which will predict the course of decay over time, for all types of tasks, as a function of the cognitive demands of the learning task, the conditions of learning, and the shape and end point of each individual's learning curve.

REFERENCES

Adams, J.A. (1983). On integration of the verbal and motor domains. In R.A. Magill (Ed.), *Memory and control of action* . Amsterdam: North-Holland.

Adams, J.A. (1985). *Historical review of research on the learning, retention, and transfer of human motor skills.* Unpublished manuscript. University of Illinois, Dept. of Psychology, Urbana-Champaign.

Ammons, R.B., Farr, R.G., Bloch, E., Neumann, E., Dey, M., Marion, R., & Ammons, C.H. (1958). Long-term retention of perceptual-motor skills. *Journal of Experimental Psychology, 55*, 318-328.

Anderson, J.R. (1976). *Language, memory, and thought.* Hillsdale, NJ: Erlbaum.

Anderson, J.R. (1982). Acquisition of a cognitive skill. *Psychological Review, 89*, 369-406.

Anderson, J.R., & Reder, L.M. (1979). An elaborative processing explanation of depth of processing. In L.S. Cermak & F.I.M. Craik (Eds.), *Levels of processing in human memory.* Hillsdale, N.J.: Erlbaum.

Annett, J. (1979). Memory for skill. In M.M. Gruneberg and P.E. Morris (Eds.), *Applied problems in memory.* London: Academic Press.

Ausubel, D.P. (1960). The use of advance organizers in the learning and retention of meaningful material. *Journal of Educational Psychology, 51*, 267-272.

Baddeley, A.D. (1978). The trouble with levels: A reexamination of Craik and Lockhart's framework for memory research. *Psychological Review, 85*, 139-152.

Bahrick, H.P. (1979). Maintenance of knowledge: Questions about memory we forgot to ask. *Journal of Experimental Psychology: General, 108*, 296-308.

Bahrick, H.P. (1984). Sementic memory content in permastore: Fifty years of memory for Spanish learned in school. *Journal of Experimental Psychology: General, 113* , 1-29.

Baldwin, R.D., Cliborn, R.E., & Foskett, R.J. (1976). *The acquisition and retention of visual aircraft recognition skills.* Report No. 76-A-4. Alexandria, VA: Army Research Institute for the Behavioral and Social Sciences.

Barnes, B.R., & Clawson, E.U. (1975). Do advance organizers facilitate learning? Recommendations for further research based on an analysis of 32 studies. *Review of Educational Rearch, 45*, 637-659.

Bartlett, F.C. 1932). *Remembering: A study in experimental and social psychology.* London: Cambridge University Press.

Battig, W.F. (1972), Intratask interference as a source of facilitation in transfer and retention. In R.F. Thompson & J.F. Voss (Eds.),. *Topics in learning & performance.* New York: Academic Press.

Battig, W.F. (1979), The flexibility of human memory. In L.S. Cermark & F.I.M. Craik (Eds.), *Levels of processing in human memory.* Hillsdale, NJ; Erlbaum.

Biel, W.C., & Force, R.C. (1943). Retention of nonsense syllables in intentional and incidental learning. *Journal of Experimental Psychology, 32*, 52-63.

Bower, G.H. (1970). Imagery as a relational organizer in associative learning. *Journal of Verbal Learning and Verbal Behavior, 9*, 529-533.

Bower, G.H. (1972). Mental imagery and associative learning. In L.W. Gregg (Ed.), *Cognition in learning and memory.* New York: Wiley.

Bower, G.H., & Karlin, M.B. (1974). Depth of processing of faces and recognition memory. *Journal of Experimental Psychology, 103*, 751-757.

Bransford, J.D., & Johnson, M.K. (1972). Contextual prerequisites for understanding: Some investigations of comprehension and recall. *Journal of Verbal Learning and Verbal Behavior, 11*, 717-726.

Carey, S.T., & Lockhart, R.S. (1973). Encoding differences in recognition and recall. *Memory and Cognition, 1*, 297-300.

Chi, M.T.T., Glaser, R., & Farr, M.J. (Eds.) (in press). *The nature of expertise.* Hillsdale, NJ: Erlbaum.

Christiaansen, R.E. (1980). Prose memory: Forgetting rates for memory codes. *Journal of Experimental Psychology: Human Learning and Memory, 6*, 611-619.

Cofer, C.N., Chmielewski, D.L., & Brockway, J.F. (1976). Constructive processes and the structure of human memory. In C.N. Coffer (Ed.), *The structure of human memory.* San Francisco: W.H. Freeman.

Conrad, R. (1967). Interference or decay over short retention intervals? *Journal of Verbal Learning and Verbal Behavior, 6*, 49-54.

Craik, F.I.M. (1979). Human memory. *Annual Review of Psychology, 30*, 63-102.

Craik, F.I.M., & Lockhart, R.S. (1972). Levels of processing: A framework for memory research. *Journal of Verbal Learning and Verbal Behavior, 11,* 671-684.

Craik, F.I.M., & Tulving, E. (1975). Depth of processing and the retention of words in episodic memory. *Journal of Experimental Psychology: General, 104,* 268-294.

Cronbach, L.J., & Snow, R.E. (1976). *Aptitudes and instructional methods.* New York: Irvington.

D'Ydewalle, G., & Lens, W. (Eds.) 1981). *Cognition in human motivation and learning .* Louwain, Belguim: Leuven University Press.

Ebbinghaus, H. (1913). *Memory: A contribution to experimental psychology* (H.A. Ruger & C.E. Bussenius, Trans.) New York: Columbia University. (Original work published 1885.)

Eysenck, M.W. (1979). Depth, elaboration, and distinctiveness. In L.S. Cermak & F.I.M. Craik (Eds.), *Levels of processing in human memory.* Hillsdale, NJ: Erlbaum.

Flexser, A.J., & Tulving, E. (1978). Retrieval independence in recognition and recall. *Psychological Review, 85,* 153-171.

Gagne, E.D. (1978). Long-term retention of information following learning from prose. *Review of Educational Research, 48,* 629-665.

Gagne, E.D., Bell, M.S., Yarbrough, D.B., & Weidemann, C. (1985). Does familiarity have an effect on recall independent of its effect on original learning? *Journal of Educational Research, 79,* 41-45.

Gagne, R.M. (in press). *Research on learning and retaining skills.* (AFHRL Tech. Report.) San Antonio: Air Force Human Resources Laboratory.

Galambos, J.A., & Rips, L.J. (1982). Memory for routines. *Journal of Verbal Learning and Verbal Behavior, 21,* 260-281.

Gardlin, G.R., & Sitterley, T.E. (1972). *Degradation of learned skills: A review and annotated bibliography* (D180-15081-1, NASA-CR-128611). Seattle, WA: Boeing Company.

Gentner, D. (1980). *The structure of analogical models in science.* Technical Report 4451. Cambridge, Ma: Bolt Beranek & Newman, Inc.

Gentner, D. (1982). Are scientific analogies metaphors? In D.S. Miall (Ed.), *Metaphor: Problems and perspectives.* Brighton, Sussex, England: Harvester Press, Ltd.

Gettlinger, M. & White, M.A. (1979). Which is the stronger correlate of school learning? Time to learn or measured intelligence? *Journal of Educational Psychology, 71,* 405-412.

Glass, G.V. (1977). Integrated findings: The meta-analysis of research. *Review of Research in Education, 5,* 351-379.

Grimsley, D.L. (1969). *Acquisition, retention and retraining: Effects of high and low fidelity in training devices.* (HumRRO Technical Report 69-1.) Alexandria, VA: Human Resources Research Office.

Hagman, J.D. & Rose, A.M. (1983). Retention of military tasks: A review. *Human Factors, 25,* 199-213.

Hall, E.R., Ford, L.H., Whitten, T.C., & Plyant, L.R. (1983). *Knowledge retention among graduates of basic electricity and electronics schools* . Technical Report 149, Orlando, FL: Training Analysis and Evaluation Group, Department of the Navy (AD-A131855)

Hiew, C.C. (1977). Sequence effects in rule learning and conceptual generalization. *American Journal of Psychology, 90,* 207-218.

Higbee, K.L., & Kunihira, S. (1985). Cross-cultural applications of Yodai mnemonics in education. *Educational Psychologist, 20,* 57-64.

Hirsch, R. (1974). The hippocampus and contextual retrieval of information from memory: A theory. *Behavioral Biology, 12,* 421-444.

Horton, D.L., & Mills, C.B. (1984). Human learning and memory. *Annual Review of Psychology, 35,* 361-394.

Hurlock, R.E., & Montague, W.E., (1982). *Skill retention and its implications for navy tasks: An Analytical Review.* NPRDC SR 82-21, San Diego, CA: Navy Personnel Research & Development Center.

Hutchins, E.L., Hollan, J.D., & Norman, D.A. (1985). *Direct manipulation interfaces.* (ICS Report 8503.) LaJolla: University of California.

Jackson, G.B. (1980). Methods for integrative reviews. *Review of Educational Research, 50,* 438-460.

Jones, M.B. (1985). *Nonimposed overpractice and skill retention.* (Contract No. MDA 903-83-K-0246.) Alexandria, VA: Army Research Institute for the Behavioral and Social Sciences.

Keppel, G. & Underwood, B.J. (1962). Proactive inhibition in short-term retention of single items. *Journal of Verbal Learning and Verbal Behavior, 1,* 153-161.

Kerr, B. (1973). Processing demands during mental operations. *Memory and Cognition, 1,* 401-412.

Kieras, D.E. (1981). *Knowledge representation in cognitive psychology* . (Contract No. N00014-78-C-0509.) Personnel and Training Research Programs, Office of Naval Research. (Tech. Report No. 7.)

Kieras, D.E., & Bovair, S. (1984). The role of a mental model in learning to operate a device. *Cognitive Science, 8,* 255-273.

Kilpatrick, J. (1985). Doing mathematics without understanding it: A commentary on Higbee and Kunihira. *Educational Psychologist, 20,* 65-68.

Kintsch, W. (1968). Recognition and free recall of organized lists. *Journal of Experimental Psychology, 78,* 481-487.

Kintsch, W. (1974). *The representation of meaning in memory.* Hillsdale, NJ: Erlbaum.

Kintsch, W. (1975). Memory representations of text. In R.L. Solso (Ed.), *Information processing and cognition.* Hillsdale, NJ: Erlbaum.

Klein, K. & Saltz, E. (1976). Specifying the mechanisms in a levels-of-processing approach to memory. *Journal of Experimental Psychology: Human Learning and Memory, 2,* 671-679.

Konoske, P.J. & Ellis, J.A. (1985, April). *Cognitive factors in learning and retention of procedural tasks.* Paper presented at the meeting of the American Educational Research Association, Chicago, IL.

Krueger, W.C.F. (1929). The effect of overlearning on retention. *Journal of Experimental Psychology, 12,* 71-78.

Kuhlmann, F. (1906). On the analysis of the memory consciousness: A study in the mental imagery and memory of meaningless visual forms. *Psychological Review, 13,* 316-348.

Kulik, J.A., Kulik, C.C., & Cohen, P.A. (1980). Effectiveness of computer-based college teaching: a meta-analysis of findings. *Review of Educational Research, 50,* 525-544.

Kunen, S., Green D., & Waterman, D. (1979). Spread of encoding effects within the nonverbal visual domain. *Journal of Experimental Psychology: Human Learning and Memory, 5,* 574-584.

Lane, N.E. (in press). *Skill acquisition curves: An analysis of applicability to the time course and sequencing of military training* . IDA Paper. Alexandria, VA: Institute for Defense Analyses.

Loftus, E.F., & Palmer, J.C. (1974). Reconstruction of automobile destruction: An example of the interaction between language and memory. *Journal of Verbal Learning and Verbal Behavior, 13,* 585-589.

Loftus, G.R. (1985). Evaluating forgetting curves. *Journal of Experimental Psychology: Learning, Memory, and Cognition, 11*, 397-406.

Luh, C.W. (1922). The conditions of retention. *Psychological Monographs,* Whole No. 142, Vol. XXXI, No. 3.

Mandler, G. (1968). Association and organization: Facts, fancies and theories. In T.R. Dixon & D.L. Horton (Eds.), *Verbal behavior and general behavior theory.* Englewood Cliffs, NJ: Prentice-Hall.

Mayer, R.E. (1975). Different problem-solving competencies established in learning computer programming with and without meaningful models. *Journal of Educational Psychology, 67,* 725-734.

Mayer, R.E. (1979). Can advance organizers influence meaningful learning? *Review of Educational Research, 49,* 371-383.

McGeoch, J.A., & Irion, A.L. (1952). *The psychology of human learning .* 2nd edition. New York: Longmans, Green and Co.

Melton, A.W. (1963). Implications of short-term memory for a general theory of memory. *Journal of Verbal Learning and Verbal Behavior, 2,* 1-21.

Merrill, M.D. (1975). Learner control: Beyond aptitude-treatment interactions. *A.V. Communications Review, 23,* 217-226.

Merrill, M.D. (1980). Learner control in computer-based learning. *Computers and Education, 4,* 77-95.

Mishkin, M. & Petri, H.L. (1984). Memories and habits: Some implications for the analysis of learning and retention. In L. Squire & N. Butters (Eds.), *Neuropsychology of memory.* New York: Guilford Press.

Mistler-Lachman, J. (1974). Depth of comprehension and sentence memory. *Journal of Verbal Learning and Verbal Behavior, 13,* 98-106.

Modrick, J.A., Levitt, R.A. Alden, D.G., & Henke, A.J. (1975). Review of approaches to cognitive style and implications for human information processing in command and decision situations. *Proceedings of the Human Factors Society, 19th Annual Meeting,* Dallas, TX.

Montague, W.E., & Wulfeck, W.H. (1984). Computer-based instruction: Will it improve instructional quality? *Training Technology Journal, 1,* 4-19.

Morris, C.D., Stein, B.S., & Bransford, J.D. (1979). Prerequisites for the utilization of knowledge in recall of prose passages. *Journal of Experimental Psychology: Human Learning and Memory, 5,* 253-261.

Naylor, J.C. & Briggs, G.E., (1961). *Long-term retention of learned skills: A review of the literature*. ASD TR 61-390. Columbus, Ohio: Ohio State University, Laboratory of Aviation Psychology.

Neisser, V. (1976). *Cognition and reality: Principles and implications of cognitive psychology*. San Francisco: Freeman.

Nelson, T.O. (1977). Repetition and depth of processing. *Journal of Verbal Learning and Verbal Behavior, 16,* 151-172.

Norman, D.A., & Bobrow, D.G. (1976). On the role of active memory processes in perception and cognition. In C.N. Cofer (Ed.), *Structure of human memory*. San Francisco: W.H. Freeman and Company.

Norman, D.A., & Bobrow, D.G. (1979). Descriptions: An intermediate stage in memory retrieval. *Cognitive Psychology, 11,* 107-123.

Oakley, D.A. (1981). Brain mechanisms of mammalian memory. *British Medical Bulletin, 37,* 175-180.

O'Keefe, J. & Nadel, L. (1978). *The hippocampus as a cognitive man*. Oxford: Clarendon Press.

Owens, J., Bower, G.H., & Black, J.B. (1979). The "soap opera" effect in story recall. *Memory and Cognition, 7,* 185-191.

Postman, L., & Senders, V.L. (1946). Incidental learning and generality of set. *Journal of Experimental Psychology, 36,* 153-165.

Prophet, W.W. (1976). *Long-term retention of flying skills: A review of the literature*. (HumRRO Final Report 76-35.) Alexandria, VA: Human Resources Research Organization (ADA036077)

Reigeluth, C.M. (1979). TICCIT to the future: Advances in instructional theory for CAI. *Journal of Computer-Based Instruction, 6,* 40-46.

Rigg, K.E. (1983). *Optimization of skill retention in the U.S. Army through initial training analysis and design*. (Contract No. DABT60-82-Q-0022.) Monterey, CA: McFann-Gray & Associates. (ADA 132188)

Rigg, K.E., & Gray, B.B. (1981). *Estimating skill training and retention functions through instructional model analysis*. (Contract MDA 903-79-C-0278.) Alexandria, VA: U.S. Army Research Institute for the Behavioral and Social Sciences. (AD B060783)

Rigney, J.W. & Lutz, K.A. (1974). *CAI and imagery: Interactive computer graphics for teaching about invisible processes*. (ONR Technical Report No. 74.) Los Angeles, CA: University of Southern California, Department of Psychology.

Riley, M.S. (1983, April). *Instructional methods that make a difference: Structural understanding and the acquisition of problem solving skills.* Paper presented at the American Educational Research Association, Montreal, Canada.

Rose, A.M., Czarnolewski, M.Y., Gragg, F.E., Austin, S.H., Ford, P., Doyle, J. & Hagman, J.D. (1984). *Acquisition and retention of soldering skills.* (Contract MDA 903-81-C-AA01.) AIR Final Report FR88600. Washington, D.C: American Institutes for Research.

Rose, A.M., Radtke, P.H., Shettel, H.H., & Hagman, J.D. (1985). *User's manual for predicting military task retention.* Report No. AIR FR37800. Washington, D.C.: American Institutes for Research.

Rubin, D.C., (1977). Very long-term memory for prose and verse. *Journal of Verbal Learning and Verbal Behavior, 16,* 611-621.

Sachs, J.S. (1967). Recognition memory for syntactic and semantic aspects of connected discourse. *Perception and Psychophysics, 2,* 437-442.

Schank, R.C., & Abelson, R.B. (1977). *Scripts, plans, goals, and understanding.* Hillsdale, NJ: Erlbaum.

Schendel, J., Shields, J., & Katz, M. (1978). *Retention of motor skills: Review.* (Technical Paper 313.) Alexandria, VA: U.S. Army Research Institute for the Behavioral and Social Sciences.

Schendel, J.D. & Hagman, J.D. (1982). On sustaining procedural skills over a prolonged retention interval. *Journal of Applied Psychology, 67,* 605-610.

Schneider, W., Dumais, S.T., & Shiffrin, R.M. (1984). Automatic and control processing and attention. In R. Parasuraman and D.R. Davies (Eds.). *Varieties of attention.* Orlando, FL: Academic Press.

Shea, J.B., & Morgan, R.L. (1979). Contextual interference effects on the acquisition, retention and transfer of a motor skill. *Journal of Experimental Psychology: Human Learning and Memory, 5,* 179-187.

Shellow, S.M. (1923). Individual differences in individual memory. *Archives of Psychology, 10,* 64-82.

Shields, J.L., Goldberg, S.L., & Dressel, J.D. (1979). *Retention of basic soldering skills.* (Research Report 1225.) Alexandria, VA: US Army Research Insitute for the Behavioral & Social Sciences.

Shiffrin, R.M. & Schneider, W. (1977). Controlled and automatic human information processing: II. Perceptual learning, automatic attending, and a general theory. *Psychological Review, 84,* 127-190.

Shimmerlik, S.M. (1978). Organization theory and memory for prose: A review of the literature. *Review of Educational Research, 48*, 103-120.

Slamecka, N.J., & McElree, B. (1983). Normal forgetting of verbal lists as a function of their degree of learning. *Journal of Experimental Psychology: Learning, Memory, and Cognition, 9*, 384-397.

Smith, E. & Goodman, L. (1984). Understanding instructions: The role of explanatory material. *Cognition and Instruction, 1*, 359-396.

Snow, R.E. (1980). *Aptitudes and instructional methods: Research on individual differences in learning-related processes.* (Final Report 1975-1979), Aptitude Research Project, Stanford, CA: Stanford University, School of Education.

Snow, R.E. & Farr, M.J. (Eds.) (in press) *Aptitude, learning and instruction, Vol. III: Conative and affective process analyses.* Hillsdale, NJ: Erlbaum.

Stern, L.D. (1981). A review of theories of human amnesia. *Memory and Cognition, 9*, 247-262.

Stevens, A., & Steinberg, C. (1981). *Project Steamer: I. Taxonomy for generating explanations of how to operate complex physical devices* . (NPRDC Technical Note 81-21.) San Diego: Navy Personnel Research and Development Center.

Sturges, P., Ellis, J., & Wulfeck, W. (1981). *Effects of performance-oriented text upon long-term retention of factual material.* (NPRDC Tech. Rep. 81-22). San Diego: Navy Personnel Research and Development Center.

Tourangeau, R. & Sternberg, R. (1982). Understanding and appreciating metaphors. *Cognition, 11*, 203-244.

Tulving, E. (1985). How many memory systems are there? *American Psychologist, 40*, 385-398.

Tulving, E., & Weisman, S. (1975). Relation between recognition and recognition failure of recallable words. *Bulletin of the Psychonomic Society, 6*, 78-82.

Tyler, S.W., Hertel, P.T., McCallum, M.C., & Ellis, H.C. (1979). Cognitive effort and memory. *Journal of Experimental Psychology: Human Learning and Memory, 5*, 607-617.

Underwood, B.J. (1977). *Temporal codes of memories: Issues and problems.* Hillsdale, NJ: Erlbaum.

Underwood, B.J., & Keppel, G. (1963). Retention as a function of degree of learning and letter-sequence interference. *Psychological Monographs, 77* (1, Whole No. 567).

Vineberg, R. (1975). *A Study of the retention of skills and knowledge acquired in basic training.* (HumRRO TR 75-10). Alexandria, VA: Human Resources Research Organization.

Wertheim, A.H. (1985, September-October). *Some remarks on the retention of learned skills.* Paper presented at NATO Conference on Transfer of Training, Brussels, Belgium.

Wetzel, S.K., Konoske, P.J., & Montague, W.E. (1983). *Estimating skill degradation for aviation antisubmarine warfare operators (AWs): Loss of skill and knowledge following training* (NPRDC SR-83-31). San Diego: Navy Personnel Research & Development Center. (ADA129407)

Wickelgren, W.A. (1973). The long and the short of memory. *Psychological Bulletin, 80,* 425-438.

Williams, M.D., & Hollan, J.D. (1981). The process of retrieval from very long-term memory. *Cognitive Science, 5,* 87-119.

Wood, G. (1983). *Cognitive psychology: A skills approach.* Monterey, CA: Brooks/Cole.

Young, R.M. (1983). Surrogates and mappings: Two kinds of conceptual models for interactive devices. In D. Gentner & A. Stevens (Eds.), *Mental models.* Hillsdale, NJ: Erlbaum.

APPENDICES

TABLE A-1. CHARACTERIZATION OF MAJOR REVIEWS OF VARIABLES AFFECTING LONG-TERM RETENTION

Review Citation	Scope; orientation; limitations; comprehensiveness; critical gaps identified, etc.
Naylor & Briggs, 1961	123 items reviewed as related to flight skills retention, the interest being mainly in motor skills. Studies reviewed were mainly research, not operationally oriented. Although motor-skills studies were sought, authors said that most experiments they could locate had been conducted in context of verbal, rather than motor learning. Furthermore, authors also complained that most of the studies involve "relatively short retention intervals." The most important "major need" cited is the need for more research which uses "fairly extended time periods between learning and recall."
Gardlin & Sitterley, 1972	Literature survey, which included 116 studies, done as part of NASA program to investigate decay of learned skills applicable to space flight, is limited to reports "dealing with close to operational conditions." This report uses the Naylor and Briggs (1961) review (noted above) to provide a background against which the more recent literature is compared and assessed. Detailed abstracts are supplied for 21 "selected reports" which were deemed seminal, integrated or representative of the NASA operational interests and subject population. Also contains "short summaries" of the remaining 25 reports reviewed. Authors concluded that the literature has "identified the level of performance on the final training period as the primary predictor of skill retention for any given retention interval duration."
Prophet, 1976	Emphasis on flying skills. Reviews 120 reports published mostly in the late sixties and seventies, as well as discussing the Naylor and Briggs (1961) and Gardlin and Sitterley (1972)

(Table A-1 Continues)

A-1

Review Citation	Scope; orientation; limitations; comprehensiveness; critical gaps identified, etc.
Prophet, 1976 (continued)	reviews (see above). A separate annotated bibliography is included. The reports reviewed are grouped on a scale of relevancy to the retention of flight skills. Of the 120 items reviewed by Prophet, 79 were not covered in either the Naylor and Briggs (1961) or the Gardlin and Sitterley (1972) reviews, mainly because of recency. In spite of the relatively large number of studies covered, Prophet states that "only a handful deal with skills of the magnitude of complexity of aircraft piloting, and very few deal with retention time intervals similar to those of concern to the USAF (1-3 years)." Prophet agrees with the Gardlin and Sitterley overall conclusion that the best predictor of long-term retention is the highest level of skill acquired prior to the no-practice retention interval. However, Prophet asserts that the general state of knowledge about long-term retention is "inadequate to USAF current and future needs." Little is known, for example, about the retention, maintenance and retraining of higher level pilot skills that characterize the professional USAF pilot in tactical operations.
Schendel, Shields & Katz, 1978	Focus is on retention of motor skills from an "extensive literature survey of pertinent research." Some of the 145 studies cited have "little direct or obvious" relationship with the skills currently maintained within the Army; however, military-research findings are emphasized. "Conflicting data and data pertinent to a more detailed understanding of the behavioral consequences of an extended no-practice period generally were skimmed over to lend coherence to this report. In so doing, an oversimplified picture of long-term motor memory and the variables that may affect it has been sketched." Conclusions include the recommendation for more basic and applied research. The most promising target for attacking the issue of skill sustainment in the Army is that of the level of original learning, since this variable is the single most important determinant of motor retention.

(Table A-1 Continues)

Review Citation	Scope; orientation; limitations; comprehensiveness; critical gaps identified, etc.
Annett, 1979	Emphasis is on long-term memory ("weeks, months or years") of skills (as contrasted to "memory for words, scenes or events"). Purpose of this review is to generalize to real-world situations; therefore, division is made between "real-life or simulated tasks and artificial laboratory tasks." There is a fundamental difficulty in making comparative assertions across different types of tasks, because "we lack a common metric for retention..." There is at present no satisfactory theory of memory for skills. Most researchers, the author contends, have been satisfied with empirical generalizations about the effects of major variables on gross performance measures. A very major question has not been asked, viz., what exactly is forgotten when complex skilled performance decays over time? Modern theories of memory may have more explanatory value, since they are concerned with the problem of coding in memory.

In general, Annett tries, wherever possible, to reinterpret prevailing views. He does this by finding methodological or paradigmatic flaws and inadequacies (lack of operational definitions) in conceptualizing variables of importance. He sometimes proposes a "cognitive" explanation for an apparently straightforward, previously noncontroversial, empirical set of findings. |
| Hurlock & Montague, 1982 | Focus is on reviewing selected research literature to identify probable variables contributing to skill loss in the Navy. Much of what is analyzed are literature reviews themselves (e.g., Naylor & Briggs, 1961; Gardlin & Sitterley, 1972; Prophet, 1976; Schendel, Shields & Katz, 1978), which the current review also includes. A total of 24 references cited (which includes the reviews) shows the relatively limited scope of this analytic review. In spite of this, the report |

(Table A-1 Continues)

A-3

Review Citation	Scope; orientation; limitations; comprehensiveness; critical gaps identified, etc.
Hurlock & Montague, 1982 (continued)	is concise and thoughtful, and pinpoints the important Navy problems involved in anticipating and reducing skill loss. It recognizes that "The most direct way to identify skill deterioration is through the use of performance-evaluation tests," but also recognizes the very practical obstacles to creating, setting up and implementing such tests. The report concludes that the scientific literature provides little information that has direct application to the problem of skill deterioration in the Navy, because: "The models upon which most of the research designs have been based are not commonly found in real jobs, and they differ dramatically from the working and learning conditions of complex working situations, e.g., the career history of Navy personnel". This report, for the most part, does not address the theoretical mechanisms underlying memory storage and retrieval, although it does acknowledge the need for further research. Its main recommendation is to develop "indirect methods" for identifying skill loss, e.g., descriptive procedures to identify conditions known to be likely to result in decay.
Hagman & Rose, 1983	Reviews 13 experiments conducted or sponsored by the Army Research Institute. These experiments mostly focus on "retention of military tasks performed in an operational environment," and examine empirical data about variables that operate to improve retention. The "conceptual framework" adopted by the report is that one can predict and control the amount and rate of K&S decay if (a) the variables influencing retention are known; and (b) we can and will pay for the probable extra resources needed (e.g., dollars, time, equipment, personnel). Three possible approaches to improving LTR are discussed. One approach is to modify the task (e.g., through equipment redesign). A second is to select for training those people who possess abilities that make it more

(Table A-1 Continues)

A-4

Review Citation	Scope; orientation; limitations; comprehensiveness; critical gaps identified, etc.
Hagman & Rose, 1983 (continued)	likely they will learn and retain the particular task skills involved. The third approach, that of improving retention through influencing the training process, is the one emphasized in the Hagman & Rose review. The review does not provide specific statistical information, although "the data from each experiment have been subjected to rigorous statistical analysis. Only those findings significant at the $p < 0.05$ level are reported." The research reported addresses only three categories of issues: training, task, and ability. For each issue, after the summary of research findings, suggested related topics for future investigation are given. Although the review states it has answered many questions of interest, it admits that "many more questions remain unanswered."

TABLE A-2. CONCLUSIONS FROM MAJOR REVIEWS OF VARIABLES AFFECTING LONG-TERM RETENTION

Operating Variable: Degree of Original Learning/Level-of-Mastery Criterion

Review Citation	Major Findings & Conclusions	Judged Strength of Effect" [Low (1) to High (5)]	Remarks
Naylor & Briggs, 1961	A. Additional amounts of original learning usually facilitates retention, but at a decreasing rate, sometimes reaching a point of no extra advantage as compared to a lesser degree of original learning.	4	A,B and C. Nearly all of the reviewed studies varying the degree of original learning used rather simple one-dimensional tasks. Authors want more complex tasks studied—they define complex as "multi-dimensional tasks requiring timesharing and coordination".
	B. It is likely that more complex tasks would also yield the same advantage, although one would also expect diminishing returns over longer retention intervals.	4	
	C. To get the improved retention resulting from overlearning of simple tasks, one would probably need considerably greater amounts of original training than are typical of "over-learning" studies.	4	
Gardlin & Sitterley, 1972	For motor tasks (predominantly tracking), skill retention varies directly with the amount of original learning (based on five studies). Authors conclude that the level of initial mastery is the main predictor of skill retention for any given interval.	3	Their conclusions do not consider the fact that complex tasks (composed of cognitive, procedural and motor components) may decay differentially as a function of the degree of original learning.

A-6

(Table 2-A Continues)

Review Citation	Major Findings & Conclusions	Judged Strength of "Effect" [Low (1) to High (5)]	Remarks
Prophet, 1976	The single most important factor in determining absolute level of performance after intervals of non-practice has consistently been found to be the level of original learning. This suggests that overlearning may benefit retention. But overlearning has not been investigated systematically for retention of complex skills such as flying.	4	Many of the flight-related studies have used arbitrarily established criterion levels that are far below those that characterize the military pilot.
Schendel, Shields & Katz, 1978	A. The single most important determinant of motor retention is level of original learning. Overlearning (what these reviewers call "overtraining" or "mastery training") can retard forgetting.	5	A. If original training needs to be extended in time, the military services must decide whether this is more feasible and cost-effective than refresher training during the no-practice retention interval.
	B. The "level" or "degree" of original learning can be increased qualitatively or reached more quickly, for motor skills, by providing diagnostically rich knowledge of results which are associated by the learner with his own reponse-produced feedback.	4	B. The benefits of an increased degree of learning extends beyond merely improved retention. Both theory and data suggest that the "overtrained" performer has more spare attentional capacity to devote to more effective time sharing or to better resist stressful environments.

A-7

(Table A-2 Continues)

Review Citation	Major Findings & Conclusions	Judged Strength of Effect" [Low (1) to High (5)]	Remarks
Annett, 1979	For both simple and complex tasks, retention is a positive, but negatively accelerated function of the amount of original learning.	4	Many of the papers leading to Annett's conclusions assert that this variable may well be the most potent influence on long-term retention.
Hurlock & Montague, 1982	A. The "amount of initial learning" is the single most important variable related to skill retention over a period of nonuse. "Any variable that leads to high initial levels of learning, such as high ability or frequent practice, will facilitate skill retention." Extensive practice during acquisition usually leads to "overlearning," and will yield greater retention because of such overlearning.	5	A. This conclusion emerges from almost all long-term K&S retention studies and reviews. If time, money and the availability of qualified personnel were not obstacles, increasing the time and practice given to initial training would probably be the single most effective way to slow down forgetting. As the current report will show, there may well be more effective/cost-effective ways of increasing the degree of original learning than by straightforwardly increasing the time allowed for learning.
	B. Although additional practice in the acquisition phase facilitates overlearning and, hence, retention, specific methods and schedules for practice have not been found to affect retention levels. Rather, the kind and quality of the practice is important: learning and retention are both enhanced when "practice approximates the functional requirements of the task."	4	B. The issue of kind and quality of practice has important implications for designing simulators for training: full physical fidelity of job and equipment cues and contexts are not necessarily going to provide best training and LTR.

A-8

(Table A-2 Continues)

Review Citation	Major Findings & Conclusions	Judged Strength of "Effect" [Low (1) to High (5)]	Remarks
Hagman and Rose, 1983	A. Three experiments on military procedural tasks, using different trainees, tasks, and criteria of mastery showed that increasing the amount of training, during or after achieving minimal task proficiency, increased retention over intervals up to 8 weeks.	4	A. The "overlearning" used ranged from three consecutive correct trials to 100% increase in number of trials to mastery. The reviewers call for additional research to determine the most cost-effective degrees of over-learning for improving the retention of different kinds of tasks.
	B. Repetition of presentation trials promotes acquisition; in contrast, repetition of <u>test</u> <u>trials fosters retention</u> (based on two experiments).	4	B. When one expects a substantial period of nonuse of a learned K or S, testing trials should be emphasized <u>during training to slow down decay.</u>

TABLE A-3. CONCLUSIONS FROM MAJOR REVIEWS OF VARIABLES AFFECTING LONG-TERM RETENTION

Operating Variable: Task Characteristics (Type, Structure, Complexity, Cognitive Demands, etc.)

Review Citation	Major Findings & Conclusions	Judged Strength of Effect" [Low (1) to High (5)]	Remarks
Naylor & Briggs, 1961	A. Found "little or no evidence that motor tasks are intrinsically less susceptible to forgetting than are verbal tasks."	2	A,B, and C. Authors realize the problem of equating types of tasks in terms of difficulty level has not been well handled. They recognize the importance of somehow taking "task organization" into account. But, because the literature they review rarely or poorly does so, their conclusions are tentative and limited in generality.
	B. Continuous tasks are better retained than discrete or procedural tasks.	4	
	C. "Task integration" or the meaningful patterning of responses may cause the retention superiority that is usually found for motor (continuous) tasks over verbal (procedural or discrete tasks).	4	
Gardlin & Sitterley, 1972	Authors viewed the level of task organization (e.g., degree of cohesiveness) as the task characteristic most influencing long-term retention. They cite five studies supporting the conclusion that the effect of task organization was strongly influenced by the degree of training: lesser trained subjects showed improved retention if they performed on a procedural task "with high organization."	4	These authors adopted their view (that the degree of task organization is the major task variable affecting retention) from the conclusion of Naylor and Briggs (1961)—see above—re: "task integration."
Prophet, 1976	Continuous control (motor) tasks are retained well, even for extended time periods, because they typically have a high degree of internal organization. Procedural tasks (such as those peculiar to flying) which lack internal organization show marked and rapid decline. However, these tasks can be fairly easily retrained. Instrument flying is more difficult to retain than visual flying, probably because of its procedural-task loading.	4	The view that the combat pilot must acquire skills to process large volumes of information correctly and rapidly should be explored, Prophet says, by using such tools as the concept of residual attention, and techniques such as the use of a secondary task.

A-10

(Table A-3 Continues)

Review Citation	Major Findings & Conclusions	Judged Strength of "Effect" [Low (1) to High (5)]	Remarks
Schendel, Shields & Katz, 1978	A. Procedural tasks and individual discrete motor responses decay in a few months or less, but continuous control tasks are retained for months or years.	4	A. Most notable data in support of this come from research on piloting skills. One possible explanation for this finding: Because it is unclear what constitutes an individual trial during "continuous" task, these responses may be overlearned, and therefore retained better than discrete motor responses.
	B. Task structure and complexity, either inherent or imposed by the individual, are important characteristics influencing retention, and when learners do organize the material to learn it better, it is better retained. Thus, tasks which are inherently amenable to learner organization are _learned_ at a faster rate than less structured tasks, and are retained "at a higher level."	3	B. This superiority of more organized material over less organized material is no longer present when the K or S is highly overlearned.
Annett, 1979	A. Although the literature seems to support the widely held belief that "motor skills" are retained better than "verbal skills," we cannot be certain whether Ss are using verbal or non-verbal (e.g., visuo-spatial or kinesthetic) method of coding for learning and retention.	2	A and B. For this first finding, and the following two, Annett reinterprets commonly held viewpoints about task characteristics by finding logical flaws in definitional limits, or by imposing a cognitive explanation. As a result, we have no choice but to downgrade our rating of the "strength of effect."

A-11

(Table A-3 Continues)

Review of Citation	Major Findings & Conclusions	Judged Strength of Effect" [Low (1) to High (5)]	Remarks
Annett, 1979 (continued)	B. The literature also strongly supports the generalization that continuous tasks (such as tracking) are better retained than discrete procedural tasks. Yet we must realize that we have no way of recording the number of repetitions in continuous tracking, whereas we <u>can</u> count the number of steps in a procedure, and thus the repetitions. We therefore can "not assert that, with the degree of [task] difficulty or the amount of learning held constant, there are differences in retention between a continuous tracking task and a procedural task."	2	
	C. Along the lines of 1 and 2 above, Annett also casts doubt upon the prevailing view that more highly "organized" or "integrated" tasks are better retained. He views task organization as a way of manipulating task difficulty, and thereby the <u>degree</u> of learning (which can be achieved within a fixed-practice period or fixed number of trials).	2	C. No one, says Annett, has come up with a satisfactory way of operationally defining the organization of a task.
A-12			
Hurlock & Montague, 1982	A. The research literature clearly indicates that complex procedural skills "are highly subject to deterioration, even after only short periods of nonuse." The main memory-load in most of these tasks is what the correct next step is, rather than <u>how</u> to perform it.	5	A. Procedural tasks are the types of task military enlisted personnel are most often required to learn. Each one of the <u>individual</u> steps of a procedure may, in fact, be complex and difficult to remember.
	B. The organizational complexity and meaningfulness of a task are complex functions of the coherence and number of steps or subtasks, as well as the familiarity and memorability of the steps. As the number of steps increases, forgetting of steps increases.	4	B. As indicated just above, prediction based on an index of number of steps must be influenced by the internal difficulty of each step by itself.

(Table A-3 Continues)

Review of Citation	Major Findings & Conclusions	Judged Strength of Effect" [Low (1) to High (5)]	Remarks
Hagman & Rose, 1983	Two experiments aimed at identifying task characteristics which promote forgetting found that the best predictor of forgetting rates was the number of performance steps required by the task. In addition, soldiers generally forgot steps, within a procedural task, that were not cued by previous steps or by the equipment involved with the task. Individual task steps most likely to be omitted or performed incorrectly, after a 4-8 week nonuse period, were those (1) judged to be difficult (i.e., requiring skilled responses); (2) required at the beginning and end of the task; and (3) involving safety.	4 (for procedural tasks, especially those typical of enlisted military tasks)	Applied to a variety of common soldier tasks requiring procedural steps. However, the complexity of each individual step can vary, as opposed to the total-task complexity. There are no studies which deal with this intra-task-step complexity within a procedural-task setting. Task complexity, in a conceptual, intuitive sense, is a strong predictor of decay. But we need an operationally useful method to index the degree and kind of complexity for all types of tasks encountered in the real world as well as the classroom.

Table A-4. CONCLUSIONS FROM MAJOR REVIEWS OF VARIABLES AFFECTING LONG-TERM RETENTION

Operating Variable: Instructional Strategy/Treatment (Conditions of Learning)

Review of Citation	Major Findings & Conclusions	Judged Strength of Effect" [Low (1) to High (5)]	Remarks
Naylor & Briggs, 1961	A. Distribution of Practice: Based on five studies on motor skills, the inconclusive results reveal "no clear indication" that this variable has any real effect upon long-duration retention (although it seems to lead to faster acquisition).	No effect found	A. The verbal-learning literature, which has more clear-cut findings, was not reviewed.
	B. Part vs. Whole: The 2 studies on motor learning yield inconclusive findings.	No effect found	
Gardlin & Sitterley, 1972	Authors do not discuss effects of type of training on retention. The "training variable" of part-task vs whole-task practice was discussed within the context of the retention period. Part-task practice led to better retention when such practice was focused on the temporal aspects of procedural tasks. Whole-task practice is superior when it refers to a single task only, whereas part-task practice is better "if it refers to whole-practice of one task within a context of time-shared tasks."	Not applicable	It is unclear whether the effects of a "training variable" are the same regardless of whether such variables are introduced during or after the acquisition phase.
Prophet, 1976	Not discussed as a variable of concern.	Not applicable	

A-14

(Table A-4 Continues)

Review Citation	Major Findings & Conclusions	Judged Strength of Effect" [Low (1) to High (5)]	Remarks
Schendel, Shields & Katz, 1978	For motor learning and retention:		
	A. Augmented feedback can facilitate learning, and by increasing motivation, can also enhance performance.	4 (on learning)	A. No data on retention given.
	B. For learning procedural tasks, functional similarity between the learning and operational tasks is a necessary and sufficient condition.	4 (on learning)	B. No data on retention given.
	C. Part-task vs whole-task training is very sensitive to the complexity of the task, learner variables, amount of practice and how performance is measured, e.g., time or trial scores. There is no literature on retention which shows any differential effect of part- vs whole-task training.	No effects predictable	C. In the absence of empirical evidence, it may be more cost-effective to use the part technique, since it can employ simulators that are cheaper, more flexible, and safer.
	D. Additional test trials, without knowledge of results, given during or after acquisition, produce less errors and faster response latencies for LTR of verbal paired associates.	4	D. There is no evidence that additional test trials, without knowledge of results, enhances the retention of motor skills.
Annett, 1979	A. In the literature on massed vs distributed learning, there is "no clear superiority."	0	A and B. Training methods can rarely be tied down, says Annett, "to a limited number of readily manipulable variables, so that comparisons in the rigorous scientific sense are virtually impossible." Studies of retention per se are rare, and the evidence is "suggestive, rather than conclusive."
	B. Part- vs whole-task learning provides no clear evidence to support either side.	0	

A-15

(Table A-4 Continues)

Review Citation	Major Findings & Conclusions	Judged Strength of Effect" [Low (1) to High (5)]	Remarks
Annett, 1979 (continued)	C. On the whole, programmed learning, which usually involves intellectual, rather than motor skills, indicates that "retention is good where acquisition is good." A substantial number of studies have shown that retention is, in general, superior after programmed rather than conventional instruction. There are no retention data on adaptive learning in motor control.	4 (for verbal skills)	C. "Good" acquisition (Annett's term) should be defined as overlearning and/or high-quality learning, in the sense of understanding what has been learned so that one can reconstruct the material or skill.
Hurlock & Montague, 1982	A. We can improve LTR of complex procedural skills and information by providing the learner with memory aids (e.g., mnemonic devices and contextual cues). These aids help to organize and integrate task elements by forming mediating links among them. Certain instructional strategies, such as "labeling, organizing and categorizing," also help the student to associate apparently unrelated components of a complex task.	3	A. Aids which better organize the K and S to be learned can be explained in terms of the relationship between "meaningful" task chunks and the learner's knowledge-representation/retrieval structure. This Hurlock & Montague report does not deal with the comparative merits of varying instructional strategies. The current paper, by contrast, develops the cognitive-theoretical case for how and why various instructional strategies are effective.
	B. Feedback to the learner (which will allow him to recognize, correct and learn from his errors) is essential to learning and relearning. Since it also helps the trainee to understand and use cues associated with the task,	4	B. What we do not know about this self-generated feedback is how long someone will remember these feedback cues without other sources of knowledge of results.

A-16

(Table A-4 Continues)

Review Citation	Major Findings & Conclusions	Judged Strength of Effect" [Low (1) to High (5)]	Remarks
Hurlock & Montague, 1982 (continued)	effective knowledge of results "develops self-generated feedback (knowledge) that tells the learner how correct performance looks, feels and sounds." Therefore, because the trainee need not depend constantly upon external or task-related information, there should be superior retention.		
Hagman & Rose, 1983	A. Spacing of individual trials, in two experiments, was more effective for delayed retention than spacing of training sessions. Such spacing is also more advantageous when applied during the acquisition stage, rather than after it.	2	A. The reviewers themselves state that additional data are needed to "determine the validity" of these findings on the effects of spacing.
	B. Specially designed extension courses for field use led to improved acquisition and retention as compared to conventional training for selected combat tasks (based on one experiment, and retention intervals ranging from 7-12 weeks). The "special" course differed as follows: (1) it stressed hands-on performance; (2) a diagnostic test accompanied each lesson, which had been created by the ISD approach; and (3) lessons were designed for self-paced training.	See "Remarks" column	B. Design of the single experiment from which these findings derive does not allow us to determine which treatment variables are responsible for the superior performance.

TABLE A-5. CONCLUSIONS FROM MAJOR REVIEWS OF VARIABLES AFFECTING LONG-TERM RETENTION

Operating Variable: Retention Interval

Review Citation; Focus of Review	Major Findings & Conclusions	Judged Strength of Effect" [Low (1) to High (5)]	Remarks
Naylor & Briggs, 1961	A. Rehearsal facilitates skill retention; the greater the degree of overt activity in rehearsal, the greater the facilitation.	3	A and B. Although imaginary or covert rehearsal of a motor task can prove effective in delaying decay, there are indications that the relative efficiency of real and imaginary practice varies with the task, and varies with the degree of symbolic rehearsal. There are implications here for fidelity of devices which might be designed to provide effective practice.
	B. The poorer the functional fidelity of the rehearsal task to the originally learned task, the less beneficial is the rehearsal.	4	
Gardlin & Sitterley, 1972	A. In general, the longer the retention interval, the greater the skill loss. But the amount of decay appears to be highly task-specific, and sensitive to additional factors (such as the amount and type of training). Even after up to 2 years of no-practice on motor (usually tracking) tasks, retraining trials led to rapid relearning, typically resulting in more than a 50% savings in number of trials.	2	A & B. As indicated, the course of forgetting in the retention period is highly sensitive to types of tasks and types of training conditions. It is thus difficult to predict with any precision the rate of decay in any specific case.
	B. For procedural tasks, increasing decrements in proficiency occurred as retention-interval duration increased. Errors of commission (as opposed to omission) are the more sensitive measures of these performance decrements on both absolute and difference scores.	4	

A-18

(Table A-5 Continues)

Review Citation	Major Findings & Conclusions	Judged Strength of Effect" [Low (1) to High (5)]	Remarks
Prophet, 1976	No adequate quantitative relationships can be derived from research to date. All that one can credibly conclude is that the longer the retention interval, the greater the amount of decay. Basic flight skills can be retained fairly well for extended periods of non-flying, but enough degradation to cause concern does occur, especially for instrument and procedural skills.	4	Prophet cites several proficiency-flying studies in which practice during the retention interval led to interference (negative transfer) when pilots were retrained in a more complex aircraft.
Schendel, Shields & Katz, 1978	Retention of motor skills follows the classical curve of forgetting: viz., the absolute amount forgotten increases with time, whereas the apparent rate of forgetting declines over time.	4	The exact shape of any forgetting curve depends upon many variables; some major ones are (a) the amount of original learning or practice; (b) the retention interval; (c) the nature (complexity) of the task; and (d) activities that interfere with learning or retention.
Annett, 1979	A. The type of task, and its complexity, both for verbal and motor skills, influences the shape of the retention-curve so that "it is not possible to be precise about a curve of forgetting of the sort demonstrated by Ebbinghaus" for nonsense-syllable learning. The varying sensitivities of different measures of retention also make it unwise to base general conclusions on the	4	A. Although the point is not brought out by Annett, individual curves of forgetting may be very diverse, as compared to group forgetting curves.

A-19

(Table A-5 Continues)

Review Citation	Major Findings & Conclusions	Judged Strength of Effect" [Low (1) to High (5)]	Remarks
Annett, 1979 (Cont'd)	shapes of forgetting curves. We can conclude that more forgetting occurs as a retention period increases, unless there is practice or rehearsal during this period.		
	B. Various kinds of rehearsal can be effective in retarding skill decay, including "imaginary" practice. And skill retention may be kept "at a relatively high level by a relatively small investment in rehearsal", perhaps even only symbolic rehearsal.	3	B. Although the importance of the level of original learning must be recognized, rehearsal even after a low degree of learning may be helpful to retention.
Hurlock & Montague, 1982	A. The longer that a skill is not practiced, the greater its degradation.	5	A. A robust finding that is universally accepted. But it is so general as to be useless for practical purposes. In contrast, item B gives useful information which can be used to predict differential decay rates for different tasks.
	B. Characteristics of the task cause different skills to deteriorate at different rates. For example, complex procedural skills with multiple steps and subtasks decay rapidly (a matter of hours or days) if not used.	5	B. This finding is the basis for an ARI-sponsored development (Rose et al, 1985) of a methodology whereby U.S. Army unit personnel can rate individual tasks in terms of how rapidly they will be forgotten over nonuse periods up to one year.

(Table A-5 Continues)

A-20

Review Citation	Major Findings & Conclusions	Judged Strength of Effect" [Low (1) to High (5)]	Remarks
Hurlock & Montague, 1982 (Cont'd)	C. Practice during learning or during the retention interval can accelerate decay, rather than preventing it, if the individual is not performing correctly and is not given "adequate" feedback.	5	C. "Adequate" feedback should provide diagnostic information to the individual, so that he knows exactly where, how and why he was wrong, and can, therefore, use the information to improve future performance based on the retained K or S.
Hagman & Rose, 1983	This variable is not considered as such in this review of 13 experiments using military tasks.	N/A	N/A

TABLE A-6. CONCLUSIONS FROM MAJOR REVIEWS OF VARIABLES AFFECTING LONG-TERM RETENTION

Operating Variable: Methods for Testing Retention/Conditions of Recall

Review Citation	Major Findings & Conclusions	Judged Strength of Effect" [Low (1) to High (5)]	Remarks
Naylor & Briggs, 1961	A. The particular retention measure used can affect the degree of retention found. Therefore, authors suggest that "the criterion for evaluating retention in an experiment should always be the one that is important in the operational task."	5	A. First trial of a relearning series is sometimes not at all predictive of the "savings" found inn relearning.
	B. Skill retention is directly related to the degree to which the retention context is replicated during original learning.	5	B. One possible explanation is that there is least cue conflict and maximum positive transfer (i.e., identity) when the retrieval-time context is the same as the acquisition context.
Gardlin & Sitterley, 1972	A. Authors do not analyze any studies comparing different measures of retention. Instead, they cite one 1967 study, using astronaut tasks, which assumed a normal distribution for the parameters measured and thus allowed use of "Z" scores to be interpreted in terms of probabilities of successful retention performance. The conclusion is drawn that the use of probability estimates can be useful in answering questions that deal with the degree of confidence that may be invested in the success of a particular mission, mission phase or individual task.	Not applicable	A. These authors, whose interests lie in improving systems effectiveness, view the probability-measure technique as suitable as a final indicant of performance for systems analysis, but as "too global for use in initial skill retention analysis."
	B. In general, skill-retention measurement should be conducted in a context similar to that surrounding original learning.	3	B. Although authors do not discuss why this contextual relationship is imortant, maximum similiarity between the training and the testing environment provides the learner with a richer choice of memory-retrieval cues.

(Table A-6 Continues)

Review Citation	Major Findings & Conclusions	Judged Strength of Effect [Low (1) to High (5)]	Remarks
Prophet, 1976	Not discussed as a variable of concern.	Not applicable	
Schendel, Shields & Katz, 1978	A. In general, the savings time to relearn to original mastery criterion is more than 50% for motor skills. However, length of retraining time is much longer for (a) longer retention intervals; (b) more "difficult" tasks; and (c) procedural tasks as opposed to continuous tasks.	4	A. Relearning can, for "some motor tasks," employ "mental practice" beneficially, especially for the "cognitive, problem-solving aspects of motor learning."
	B. Highly trained individuals tend to need more retraining time than lesser-trained people to regain their original mastery level.	3	B. This apparently counter-intuitive finding concerns absolute amounts of forgetting. One should appreciate the fact that people who are highly trained have more to forget, and, therefore, more to relearn.
Annett, 1979	Typical results, cited only for motor retention (which mostly use the savings score from relearning), suggest that relearning is usually fairly rapid, even after as much as 22 months delay, with time savings up to 90%. No data or conclusions are given about other than motor learning as a task, and relearning as the measure of retention.	3 (motor skill only)	The degree of original learning is not described for the few motor studies reviewed. In motor learning, it is especially difficult to specify a meaningful mastery level: there may be unrecognized overlearning which is partly responsible for the strong savings effect found in relearning.
Hurlock & Montague, 1982	A. Recall can be facilitated by increasing the perceived similarity between the conditions or context of the recall situation and the original learning conditions.	4	A. This obviously occurs because greater similarity provides a larger number and variety of retrieval cues. This relationship is of significant importance in the fidelity-of-simulation question.

(Table A-6 Continues)

A-23

Review Citation	Major Findings & Conclusions	Judged Strength of Effect" [Low (1) to High (5)]	Remarks
Hurlock & Montague, 1982 (continued)	B. The amount of retraining needed to regain initial mastery level appears to be inversely related to the length of the non-utilization period.	3	B. Although a fairly obvious, intuitive conclusion, this simple relationship is not a one-to-one relationship in most cases, especially with complex or difficult tasks.
	C. To maintain a learned skill, one appears to need only occasional practice and short periods of rehearsal. Even practice of only one aspect of a task seems to help retard forgetting.	2	C. There is no citation given to support the assertion about practice on only one aspect of the task. If true for most tasks and periods of no practice, it has strong implications for cost-effective refresher training.
	D. Methods normally used in original learning are effective for retraining. Procedural skills, in particular, can be quickly relearned by studying written job aids or reminder material such as technical manuals.	4	D. As with C, this also has important practical implications for cost-effective refresher training.
	E. Test-taking, especially if the test is of the hands-on, performance type, can serve to provide refresher training.	3	E. Test-taking, during the retention phase, may be used as an opportunity to practice job skills or knowledge which are not usually tapped by day-to-day job demands.
Hagman & Rose, 1983	This variable is not considered as such in this review of 13 experiments using military tasks. However, the retention measure employed in most of these experiments was the relearning (savings score), wherein the first relearning trial also constituted a retention test in terms of errors or time.	N/A	N/A

TABLE A-7. CONCLUSIONS FROM MAJOR REVIEWS OF VARIABLES AFFECTING LONG-TERM RETENTION

Operating Variable: Individual Differences (e.g., ability, set, prior familiarity)

Review Citation	Major Findings & Conclusions	Judged Strength of Effect" [Low (1) to High (5)]	Remarks
Naylor & Briggs, 1961	Authors do not consider individual differences that Ss bring to the learning situation. They do deal with manipulating the state of learner by:		
	A. Motivation: They conclude that motivational factors in learning may reflect themselves in retention, at least on the simpler motor tasks;	2	A. Motivation (a non-cognitive variable) probably interacts unpredictably with individual-differences of a cognitive nature, e.g., ability.
A-25	B. Hypnosis: Effect appears positive for retention; this suggests the possibility of using hypnosis for training and retention of at least "simple procedural skills."	2	B. Hypnosis is tricky, cannot be applied uniformly to everyone, and may be dangerous for sub-clinically emotionally disturbed individuals.
Gardlin & Sitterly, 1972	Authors do not cite any work which used individual differences as a variable of interest, but assert: "Inexplicably little attention has been given to the identification of those characteristics of individuals" who learn faster or who learn more, or both. These characteristics should be related to how well the acquired knowledge or skill is retained.	Not Applicable	Authors call for further work to be done in this area.

(Table A-7 Continues)

Review Citation	Major Findings & Conclusions	Judged Strength of "Effect" [Low (1) to High (5)]	Remarks
Prophet, 1976	As with Gardlin and Sitterley (above), no work is cited which uses individual differences as a variable directly affecting retention. One study is cited which found extremely high correlations over periods of up to 24 months in pre- and post-retention interval proficiency on a continuous-control perceptual-motor task.	Not Applicable	Prophet speculates that aptitude tests might yet prove useful for predicting the rates of original acquisition, of skill decay, and skill reacquisition. However, no data are given to support this possibility.
Schendel, Shields & Katz, 1978	A. There is some evidence that more intelligent learners may acquire and retain more motor skills using whole- rather than part-training methods.	2	A. This evidence is based on only one study of Army basic trainees learning rifle marksmanship.
	B. Individual ability levels are important in affecting retention "insofar as they influence a person's time to achieve a standard level of performance." Individuals of higher initial ability tend to achieve higher levels of proficiency and retain skill at a higher level than individuals of lower initial ability. The "ability" refers to AFQT scores, for a variety of complex tasks; it also refers to the learner's early performance on a to-be-retained motor skill.	4	B. Refresher training can be shorter and less frequent for persons of higher initial ability.

(Table A-7 Continues)

Review Citation	Major Findings & Conclusions	Judged Strength of Effect" [Low (1) to High (5)]	Remarks
Annett, 1979	"There has been no systematic examination [for motor memory] of the relationships between individual difference variables, for example, age or ability, and retention variables." Since performance at the end of original learning does predict retention, and is generally positively correlated with abilities, there is some reason to believe that these abilities should, in turn, be somewhat predictive of retention.	2	Annett acknowledges that "the absence of any thorough investigation of relationships between retention and individual differences makes generalization hazardous."
Hurlock & Montague, 1982	A. Because the amount of skill retained is directly related to the amount of initial acquisition, high-ability personnel will retain more, for a fixed amount of learning time, than low-ability individuals. This is because the higher ability personnel initially learned more. However, if both low- and high-ability personnel are trained to the same mastery criterion, there will be no retention differences between the two groups. The reason is that the actual rate of forgetting is independent of the level of ability.	3	A. There is some recent evidence in the literature that the retention curve is not the same even if we start from the same level of mastery (see Loftus, 1985).
	B. Aging does produce progressive, gradual declines in physical strength and endurance, as well as in short-term memory. However, probably because experience and knowledge bring compensatory activities into the picture, there is no significant decrease in skill retention during the age range of concern to the military.	4	B. It is probable that certain complex cognitive tasks will show less decay caused by aging than simple verbal tasks or perceptual-motor/motor tasks. This is so because there is more leeway in the complex cognitive task for the experience and abilities of the aging individual to allow compensating facilitative strategies to operate.

(Table A-7 Continues)

A-27

Review Citation	Major Findings & Conclusions	Judged Strength of Effect" [Low (1) to High (5)]	Remarks
Hagman & Rose, 1983	A. Findings of two experiments tells us that general ability factors mainly affect acquisition: Smarter trainees learn faster than low-ability personnel. If training time is equal for both kinds, those of high ability will reach higher acquisition levels. This superiority persists over time. However, the "rate of forgetting is the same, regardless of the ability level."	3	A. Given the conclusion about the rate of decay, it follows that if both ends of the ability spectrum learn to the same degree of mastery, they will show equal retention. The reviewers acknowledge that additional research is needed "to substantiate this notion."
	B. Training methods and ability levels (based on scores derived from the Armed Services Vocational Aptitude Battery) interact to yield differences in acquisition. Higher-ability soldiers, in general, gain more from self-paced, individualized instruction. In contrast, the lower-ability trainees tend to improve their acquisition more from group-paced classroom instruction.	2	B. Note that this finding applies only to the acquisition stage. However, prior research by Vineberg (1975) on soldiers of varying ability levels suggest that differences in acquisition due to ability differences are maintained over intervals of nonuse. At any rate, these findings clearly suggest that we must include both training method and ability level in predicting acquisition and retention.

A-28

TABLE B-1. REVIEW OF FACTORS INFLUENCING LONG-TERM KNOWLEDGE AND SKILL RETENTION

REFERENCE: Grimsley, D.L. (1969)

BASIS FOR CONCLUSION: Experimental Manipulation of Fidelity of Simulation for Acquiring Complex Procedural Skill

Type of Task	Task Characteristics	Level of Initial Acquis (Mastery Crit)	Type/Conditions of LRNG (INST STRATEG)	Retention Interval(s)	Ind. Diffs in Learners	Retraining Conditions	Remarks/Results/Conclusions/ Limitations, etc.
Operate the section control indicator console of the Nike-Hercules guided-missile system during both preparation and firing status.	92 step procedural task	One errorless trial. (Time was not a factor.) Score was number of steps performed correctly.	Ss trained individually on one of three panels differing in appearance and/or functional fidelity.	Four (4) and six (6) weeks	N/A	After the 6-week test, Ss were corrected on errors made, and continued until they had reached criterion of performing 90% of steps correctly. Time and number of trials to reach criterion were scored.	FOCUS: Does training by low-and high-fidelity simulators lead to differences in long-term retention and retraining? APPROACH: 60 trainees in Advanced Individual Training from the U.S. Army Training Center were trained to perform task on one of three devices differing in fidelity: (a) a functioning duplicate of the tactical equipment (b) a non-functioning duplicate of the tactical equipment and (c) a full-size artist's renroduction painted to resemble the illuminated panel. RESULTS: No significant differences found in initial training proficiency, amounts remembered at either interval, or retraining time as a function of level of simulation. CONCLUSION: The fidelity of training simulators for procedural tasks can be quite low with no adverse effect on acquisition, retention, or time to retrain.

B-1

TABLE B-2. REVIEW OF FACTORS INFLUENCING LONG-TERM KNOWLEDGE AND SKILL RETENTION

REFERENCE: Schendel, J. D. & Hagman, J. D. (1982)

BASIS FOR CONCLUSIONS: Experiments with 42 U.S. Army reservists

Type of Task	Task Characteristics	Level of Initial Acquis (Mastery Crit)	Type/Conditions of LNG (INST STRATEG)	Retention Interval(s)	Ind. Diffs in Learners	Retraining Conditions	Remarks/Results/Conclusions/ Limitations, etc.
Procedural	35-step procedure in disassembly/assembly of machine gun	(1) One errorless trial (minimal mastery) (2) 100% overtraining (overlearning), i.e., double the number of trials to reach minimal mastery	Time at which the "extra" trials, i.e., those constituting overlearning, are introduced: (a) As an immediate continuation of the acquisition phase (b) 4 weeks after acquisition and 4 weeks before retention test.	4 weeks and 8 weeks	All 3 groups had similar amounts of pre-experimental experience on the experimental task.	Same as initial acquisition	FOCUS: (1) What is the effect of "over-learning," no matter when it occurs, on retention? (2) What is the effect of "spacing" or introducing the "overlearning trials" at a point sometime during a no-practice retention interval? APPROACH: Traditional "overlearning" group compared by delayed retention test to an equated group which receives the same percent of "overlearning trials," but receives them halfway during the re-tention period (as opposed to the extra trials being contiguous with the acquisition trials). RESULTS: (1) Both "overlearning groups" made significantly fewer errors than control group in the retention test (2) The traditional overlearning group retained the material "marginally better" than did the group who received the "extra" trials midway through the 8-weeks retention period. CONCLUSIONS: (1) The amount of training (degree of learning) provided is far more important for learning and retention than is the time at which that training is introduced. "Overtraining may be a potent avenue for reducing costs and in-creasing effectiveness, at least when sustaining procedural skills over a fixed retention interval."

REFERENCE: Wertheim, A. H. (1985)

BASIS FOR CONCLUSION: Experimental study with military and non-military subjects

Type of Task	Task Characteristics	Level of Initial Acquis (Mastery Crit)	Type/Conditions of LNG (INST STRATEG)	Retention Interval(s)	Ind. Diffs in Learners	Retraining Conditions	Remarks/Results/Conclusions/ Limitations, etc.
Sequential performance involved in shooting down enemy aircraft in a simulated radar-aided anti-aircraft weapon system	Sequence of subtasks, none of which "requires any particular sensory or motor skill beyond own natural capabilities, e.g., pushing a button or pulling a switch"	Both groups had received the same standard initial training and had had the same high level of experience.	Acquired skills by regular Dutch armed service training and on-job experience (no other information given)	1 year	N/A	No retraining given	APPROACH: Experimental group (ex-conscripts who had been out of service for one year) was compared by performance tests to control group which was equally well trained and experienced, but still on active duty. RESULTS: "No loss of skill on any of the subtasks, neither on the performance scores nor on the time to perform them." CONCLUSION (by author): Training had been focussed on cognitive factors, i.e., on rules that, once learned, are hard to forget. "Our conclusion is that, if a task solely consists of such basic requirements, we need only to train its cognitive aspects, and if they are not too complex, we need not worry about forgetting. (My comment: The reason for no apparent forgetting in this situation is, perhaps, learning with understanding had given the experimental group the ability to instantly regenerate the responsive behaviour.)

TABLE B-4. REVIEW OF FACTORS INFLUENCING LONG-TERM KNOWLEDGE AND SKILL RETENTION

REFERENCE: Wetzel, Konoske & Montague (May 1983)

BASIS FOR CONCLUSION: Experimental data on Navy personnel

Type of Task	Tasks and Task Characteristics	Level of Initial Acquis (Mastery Crit)	Type/Conditions of LRG (INST STRATEG)	Retention Interval(s)	Ind. Diffs in Learners	Retraining Conditions	Remarks/Results/Conclusions/ Limitations, etc.
SONAR signal processing for Naval Aviation Antisubmarine (ASW) Warfare operators (analyze/classify acoustically-sensed information which is usually displayed).	Acoustic analysis procedures which first require learning an "extensive, complicated knowledge base." Authors divided task into: (a) Knowledge factors; (b) Computational skills; and (c) Gram-analysis procedures.	Regular final exam for Navy course to provide "Basic training in methods of acoustic analysis, integration of acoustic intelligence information, and target-classification procedures." This test Included: factual items & computational items & a performance subtest on static linear lofargrams.	Learning during 4-week training at Common Core Acoustic Analysis School for S-3A training pipeline (Aviation ASW operators in AW rating).	Approximately 1 month	N/A	None	APPROACH: Ss were 20 AWs who attended 4-week initial training, followed by operator course. Between the two courses is a 25-day period when skills are not practiced. Retention test was alternate forms of the original measure. RESULTS: Significant degradation of knowledge factors, computational skills and gram-analysis procedures. CONCLUSIONS: The complex nature of the skills involved here probably accounted for the significant skill loss. When there is going to be any unpreventable delay between finishing one course and starting a follow-on course, students need to be given the opportunity and motivation to practice their newly learned skills during the transition period between schools. If practice can't be provided during the transition, then refresher training should be built into the curriculum of the follow-on school. See also chart on Hall, Ford, Whitten & Plyant (1982) for a related Navy-context study built around a complex task-type (viz., DC and AC theory).

TABLE B-5. REVIEW OF FACTORS INFLUENCING LONG-TERM KNOWLEDGE AND SKILL RETENTION

REFERENCE: Shields, Goldberg & Dressel (1979)

BASIS FOR CONCLUSION: Experiment with soldiers

Type of Task	Task Characteristics	Level of Initial Acquis (Mastery Crit)	Type/Conditions of LNG (INST STRATEG)	Retention Interval(s)	Ind. Diffs in Learners	Retraining Conditions	Remarks/Results/Conclusions/ Limitations, etc.
20 Common Soldier tasks	Included: reporting enemy information, loading and firing grenade launcher, donning gas mask, & CPR (mostly hands-on procedural-task steps)	Completion of regular Army initial (basic) training	N/A	Ranged from 4 - 12 months following initial basic training for 523 soldiers	N/A	N/A	FOCUS: Types of tasks or task characteristics as they relate to skill and knowledge deterioration over no-practice intervals. RESULTS: (1) Rate of skill decay was a function of the task; (2) Best predictor of forgetting rate was the number of performance steps that the task called for; (3) Types of steps frequently missed, across tasks, showed consistency. In general, soldiers forgot steps not cued by the equipment or by the previous steps, such as those involving safety.

B-5

TABLE B-6. REVIEW OF FACTORS INFLUENCING LONG-TERM KNOWLEDGE AND SKILL RETENTION

REFERENCE: Rigg, K. E. (1983)

BASIS FOR CONCLUSION: Study to relate selected characteristics of Army tasks to how long and how well soldiers will retain the tasks skills

Type of Task	Task Characteristics	Level of Initial Acquis (Mastery Crit)	Type/Conditions of LNG (INST STRATEG)	Retention Interval(s)	Ind. Diffs In Learners	Retraining Conditions	Remarks/Results/Conclusions/ Limitations, etc.
Army MOS-derived tasks	Procedural, and/or cognitive and/or physical, e.g., firing a machine gun, "shooting an azimuth."	Standard end-of-course test	Standard Army training of procedural tasks, involving a demonstration "talk-through" of each procedural sequence by the instructor	"Several weeks"	N/A	N/A	APPROACH: Constituted a "limited study," part of a larger study to relate acquisition levels to retention curve. It selected seven task characteristics, derived from the research literature (see Rose ... Hagman, 1984 & Hagman & Rose, 1983), as being "most often related to skill retention & decay." Each task studied was rated in terms of the extent to which these task characteristics would enhance or degrade its retention. Each "task categorization score" thus derived was correlated with an "index of task retention," which represents the amount of decay, in task proficiency between acquisition and retention.
							RESULTS: None of the correlations between task categorization scores and the retention index was significant. Correlations between task categorization scores and absolute retention score were also non-significant.
							CONCLUSION: The assignment of a task categorization rating did not include a sensitive weighting in terms of the degree to which the task properly characterized the task. Furthermore, other task variables should perhaps have been included. This study was so molar and relatively non-discriminating that its results: at the least, need further exploration. The author himself calls this a limited study, & offers possible reasons for the negative results (p. 35).

B-6

TABLE B-7. REVIEW OF FACTORS INFLUENCING LONG-TERM KNOWLEDGE AND SKILL RETENTION

REFERENCE: Baldwin, Cliborn & Foskett (1976)

BASIS FOR CONCLUSION: Experiment with U.S. Army Soldiers

Type of Task	Task Characteristics	Level of Initial Acquis (Mastery Crit)	Type/Conditions of LNG (INST STRATEG)	Retention Interval(s)	Ind. Diffs in Learners	Retraining Conditions	Remarks/Results/Conclusions/ Limitations, etc.
Visual aircraft recognition		Acquisition was measured by the gain between pretest given before training and a posttest given after training. Scoring done on basis of percent of aircraft correctly recognized.	Group-paced instruction vs. self-paced instruction	N/A (This experiment did not examine retention for each ability group.)	Groupings of low, intermediate, and high-ability soldiers based on math and verbal ability scales of the ASVAB	N/A	FOCUS: How ability level and instructional treatment influence acquisition. RESULTS: Low-ability group achieved greater gain (in percent recognized) under group-paced training than did the intermediate-ability group (13% vs 4%). However, there was an interaction in that, under self-paced instruction, the intermediate-level group was superior to the low-ability one (18% vs 11%). The two high-ability groups learned equally well by both training methods. CONCLUSIONS: The interaction between training methods and ability differences needs to be considered in predicting learning. By extrapolating these results to those obtained by Vineberg (1975) on the retention of basic training tasks after 6 weeks, one could infer that training methods might interact with ability levels to influence retention. The training method-by-ability level interaction needs further exploration with a variety of training methods (e.g., computer-assisted instruction) and a wider range of ability-level measures.

TABLE B-8. REVIEW OF FACTORS INFLUENCING LONG-TERM KNOWLEDGE AND SKILL RETENTION

REFERENCE: Hall, E. R., Ford, L. H., Whitten, T. C. and Plyant, L. R. (1983)

BASIS FOR CONCLUSION: Empirical study of knowledge loss after Navy school training

Type of Task	Task Characteristics	Level of Initial Acquis (Mastery Crit)	Type/Conditions of LNG (INST STRATEG)	Retention Interval(s)	Ind. Diffs in Learners	Retraining Conditions	Remarks/Results/Conclusions/ Limitations, etc.
Navy course in Basic Electricity and Electronics (BE/E)	Phase 1 covers DC theory; phase 2 covers AC theory	Number correct on final BE/E tests for phase 1 and phase 2	Self-paced U.S. Navy course, taught under computer-managed instruction	From 18 to 34 days	AFQT centile scores and ASVAB selector composite scores	N/A	FOCUS: Retention of knowledge (as opposed to skill) as a function of retention interval and ability of trainees. APPROACH: Trainees who had completed BE/E course were given, just before entry in the "A" School for Construction Electrician (CE), a multiple-choice final exam identical to the ones taken at the BE/E school for both DC and AC theory. (Note: BE/E training is self-paced under computer-managed instruction; CE school is not self-paced.) RESULTS: (a) Significantly greater proportion of decay found for AC theory. (b) AFQT significantly predicted the proportion of knowledge decay—the higher the AFQT, the less the decay. CONCLUSIONS: (a) Decay of a difficult/ complex knowledge domain could be decreased by raising ability-level requirements to enter the training course; (b) Since length of retention interval was the "most powerful predictor of knowledge decay", a decrease in transit time between the BE/E and the CE "A" School should reduce memory loss; (c) The findings here (about ability influencing decay rate) may be peculiar to the training material i.e., to complex knowledge, as compared to the usual procedural skills that have been studied by the military.

B-8

TABLE B-9. REVIEW OF FACTORS INFLUENCING LONG-TERM KNOWLEDGE AND SKILL RETENTION

REFERENCE: Vineberg, R. (1975)

BASIS FOR CONCLUSION: Experiments with U.S. Army soldiers

Type of Task	Task Characteristics	Level of Initial Acquis (Mastery Crit)	Type/Conditions of LRNG (INST STRATEG)	Retention Interval(s)	Ind. Diffs in Learners	Retraining Conditions	Remarks/Results/Conclusions/ Limitations, etc.
Army basic-training tasks	13 different tasks taught in Army basic training	Satisfactory completion of Army basic training	U.S. Army basic training	Six weeks after completion of basic training	Ability as measured by the mental categories II, III and IV, as identified by the AFQT	N/A	FOCUS: Relationship of individual differences (e.g., ability) in learners to acquisition and amount/rate of decay. RESULTS: A direct relationship found between mental category and overall task performance tested at end of basic training (initial acquisition), and at retention testing six weeks later in terms of mean number of tasks performed correctly. [See Figure below.] CONCLUSIONS: (a) General-ability differences primarily affect level of initial mastery; retention decay occurs at the same rate, regardless of ability. (b) Retention differences based upon ability differences can be reduced by having a common level of initial acquisition reached. (This might necessitate longer training time for low-ability Ss, or might be achieved by other instructional strategies.) See other chart on work by Baldwin, Cliborn & Foskett (1976) illustrating interaction of ability level with instructural approach for acquisition phase.